Hey Glitterbomb!

A NO-BS GUIDE TO BEING TOO MUCH, TAKING UP SPACE, AND LOVING THE LEGACY YOU CREATE

By Kari Ginsburg, CCMP, PCC

Published by Kari Ginsburg | Uproar Coaching, LLC
Edited by Katharine Mosesso
Designed by Kate Christy, Folk Founded
Author Photo by DJ Corey

ORDERING INFORMATION:
Quantity Sales: Special discounts are available on quantity purchases by corporations, educational and coursework, associations, and others. For details, email hello@uproarcoaching.com

Individual Sales: *Hey Glitterbomb!* can be ordered directly from uproarcoaching.com and is available for purchase from all major bookstores and online book sellers.

For additional facilitation support and workshops, speaking engagements, and discussion guides, contact hello@uproarcoaching.com.

ISBN 979-8-9928075-2-3

What's Inside
This Riot of a Book

For K and E and C and F and C and D

The brightest little glitterbombs worth creating a legacy for.

Sorry about the swears.

✳ Disclaimer ✳

Before we get started, real talk—this book is here to shake things loose, get you thinking, and support you as you unapologetically own your awesome. But it's not a substitute for professional advice. I'm a coach, not a therapist, doctor, or legal expert. If you need medical, psychological, financial, or legal guidance, please reach out to a qualified professional.

Also, while I share stories, insights, and more than a bit of sass, your journey is your own. While the tools and insights in this book are designed to help you step into your full, vibrant power, your results will depend on your own badassery, effort, and circumstances. Take what works, tweak what doesn't, and make it your own—because no one does *you* better than *you*.

Now, let's get to the good stuff.

*

PROLOGUE

Happy Pinky Day

In March 2012, the right side of my face started to go numb, where my cheekbone and jaw meet in front of my ear. And I thought, "Well, that's weird." But the month before I had Norovirus — the super-flu. Maybe I pinched a nerve in my face when I was sick, and it was only now recovering. I'd give it a week, maybe 10 days to settle down.

At that time, I was married with two rescue dogs and balancing a demanding career as a leader in the federal government with professional acting gigs and teaching artist work through a local school district. I was booked, busy, and busting my ass each day to do good work, make an impact, and look in the mirror at the end of very long days and know that the person who was reflected back was doing her best. A lot of people needed me in different ways for different things, and I struggled with the feeling of having to be "everything for everyone". High stress, high achievement, high output, high demand — that's me.

Yep, we swear here.

The facial numbness didn't get better. In fact, it started to spread towards my nose and then up towards my hairline and down towards the corner of my mouth. But only on the right side of my face. I would touch my face and I could see that I was smooshing it around, but I had no sensation of the touch.

I again rationalized: I had a double emergency root canal right before Christmas. Maybe something happened then, and the infection wasn't totally removed? So, I called my dentist for an exam and some x-rays. During my appointment, my dentist didn't find anything, but she did share that she recently saw a patient with similar symptoms who ended up having face Shingles. She recommended I go see my GP.

By this time, I was referring to my numb face as Numby Face.

At the beginning of April, I went to see my GP. I told her about what was happening and where I'd been so far on my diagnostic journey. She disagreed about the Shingles and sent me for blood work and referred me to a Neurologist because "maybe it's a touch of Bell's Palsy."

I got an appointment with a Neurologist, where he asked me a lot of questions about my life & lifestyle. How much do you eat? Do you drink alcohol or take recreational drugs? What is your exercise situation? How many hours do you work a day? Based on my answers, he wrote out referrals for some imaging. He agreed that it might be Bell's Palsy or a micro stroke. The scans would tell us.

Early May 2012, I had an MRI. And my Numby Face continued to spread.

On May 22, 2012, I returned to the Neurologist's office for my results. I went by myself because we all thought we knew the answer. I was sitting on the exam table trying to crinkle the paper as little as possible when he knocked on the door and said, "Hey, come with me." I followed him to his office and sat down. He turned around his monitor so that I could see it.

He said, "You have a brain tumor."

That's the day the game changed.

Before we go any further: THIS IS NOT A BRAIN TUMOR BOOK. I'm sharing this because I want you to know this about me, because it's a foundational moment that allowed me to say HELL YES to me, all of me. I'm sharing this because if you're looking for permission to choose you, here it is. The rest of this book is going to offer you tools and thought exercises so that you can unapologetically and unabashedly choose yourself, too, without waiting for your proverbial tumor to show you what's important.

Where was I? Oh. Yes.

I literally don't remember what else he said, because a high-pitched siren went off in my head. Self-preservation mode kicked in, though, because I took notes in handwriting that doesn't look like mine. It was a big tumor, nestled behind my right ear. It was pushing against my facial nerve, hence the numbness. I needed to see a Neurosurgeon immediately. And an audiologist and ophthalmologist, and an oncologist. Things I must have done: thanked him. Taken my pile of referrals. Stopped at the counter and handed over my co-pay. Left the building and went to my car.

I *do* remember pep-talking myself on this short walk, "hold it together, 15 more feet, pop the locks, close the car door, breathe." Once I was inside the car, I broke.

I cried from fear. I cried from anger. I mourned who I was before, and I grieved for the life I thought I wouldn't have anymore.

I cried and I cried, and I cried.

I named my brain tumor Pinky, like from Pinky and the Brain.

And then I got to work. Well, we got to work. I told people who I thought could hold the experience with me, who could be my support team. I got a second opinion, and did my pre-op appointments, and my insurance and intake paperwork, and my partner and I got some really necessary legal documentation in order so that he would be protected if something even more catastrophic happened.

On July 8, 2012, I had brain surgery because other forms of treatment weren't available due to Pinky's size and placement, and the progression of my symptoms; things were… not good. Three days later, I was released from the hospital to begin recovering at home. I had PT and OT, and I requested mental health support. I was set to return to work *eight weeks* later.

During those eight weeks, I had a lot of time to think about what was really worth it, what I valued, and who I wanted to be coming out of this experience. It made me come to terms with where I wanted to work and where I wanted to work hard. I had to learn how to do certain things all over again, because my balance was shot, I had muscle paralysis on the right side of my face, and I lost the hearing in my right ear. I had mental hurdles that I had to get over, not trusting my body.

Pinky changed me. I was changing. In fact, one-half to two-thirds of people who are exposed to some form of trauma experience post-traumatic change or growth — their experiences spark a fundamental shift (Collier, 2016).

Since my energy was so limited, I stopped being who I thought I was supposed to be and embraced my prismatic self. I had an electrifying new clarity of purpose. My values of kindness, empathy, and play were my tripod for strength. That's all there was room for, and it was way more than enough.

Let's be clear: you don't need a brain tumor to have a breakthrough. Pinky was mine. Yours might be a breakup, a breakdown, a job loss, a moment of burnout so intense it left you gasping, or just waking up one day so bone-tired of your own bullshit that something has to change. Everyone has a moment that shakes the snow globe of their life and dares them to watch where the glitter settles. It doesn't have to be catastrophic to be catalytic. This book isn't about trauma — it's about transformation. And every glitterbomb I've ever worked with has had their moment. This is your opportunity.

And for me? Well, Pinky cracked everything open. But to really understand how I rebuilt from there — to see why I do the work I do now — we've got to rewind a little.

After graduating from Syracuse University with a degree in theater and a solid understanding of the human condition, I went looking for a job. Thus, Business Kari was created and she was the greatest acting role of my life. She dressed in a very elder-millennial, business casual way. She wore her long curly brown hair in a workplace-appropriate coiffure. She wasn't overly showy with piercings or makeup or jewelry, although she was delightfully flashy with her footwear. Business Kari even had a business voice and a business presence. And Business Kari was miserable. Quite honestly, IRL Kari was miserable too.

Don't worry. I'm going to get really annoying about this in a couple of chapters.

She — I — was miserable because I was forcing myself to conform my approach to work, my style of leading, and my way of representing myself in the world in a way that was completely inauthentic. I was mentored to tone down my colorfulness. Where I worked, there were unspoken rules about not standing out due to anything but performance, and only then was it appropriate to stand out because of high performance.

My leadership style had to be like my peers'. My problem solving needed to follow the models of the primarily white men who have published business books on how to lead and be successful. Thing is, those dudes have decades on me, they don't look or think like me, and their experiences came from a really profound place of privilege that was unlike my own lived experience. There's this belief that if you don't lead the way they prescribe, you're obviously doing it wrong. Like so many of us, I tried to emulate them and put their prescribed plans into action, and every day I was acutely aware that the male/pale/stale way of doing things was holding me back.

Before Pinky, I didn't know how to speak up for myself or who to reach out to for nontraditional mentorship, coaching and guidance. I was afraid that by asking I would be admitting that I was an imposter, unqualified or undeserving of my achievements. When I looked around, I could see the other non-traditional leaders like me becoming more beige with each passing day. Their presence, voices, and expertise diminished because they approached things in new or unconventional ways, too. These new ways threatened the navy suits/ neutral tie chuckleheads.

I'm probably gonna use this again and shorten it to FFS. Just so you know.

Like so many before me, I was encouraged to:

- Take up less space — Be small, fit in and don't make a mess
- Speak quietly — Conduct polite conversation in agreeable tones and cede thought-leadership to those who have legacy places at the table
- Act more like a man — for fuck's sake, this one boils my blood. It's absolute, patriarchal, misogynistic bullshit
- Downplay my authentic self — Don't be who you are, be who we want you to be

I was expected to shrink myself until the conform-ing was complete and I was a soft-focus, much-diluted shell of myself. Only then could I too assume a seat at the table.

And it's a shame. It took a scary diagnosis for me to crawl out of the hole I shoved myself into and to truly *own* that I'm less conventional than what's "expected".

Post-Pinky and those eight resetting and reclaiming weeks, I finally breathed my true self into my work and my interactions with those around me in the various roles I was playing-at instead of living-as, my ability to get things done exploded.

Once I let go of someone else's way of doing things, I *felt* better in my own skin.

Instead of taking up less space, or being quiet, or downplaying my true self, I became MORE of me. I began dressing in a way that reflected my style. I spoke up with confidence and built coalitions of other unconventional women and gender diverse leaders — whom I call glitterbombs — in an effort to spark bold change. I let go of who I thought I needed to be and embraced who I was. And then I turned up the glorious volume. I became, vivaciously, me. In doing so:

Coincidentally, this is what sparked my coaching journey.

- I was sought after for cross-government people-focused tiger teams, to improve workplace culture and how we fiercely champion the people experience for staff,

- I was recruited to lead a small-yet-mighty change management team that had global reach,

- I achieved professional-level coaching certification in record time, and then was honored as both a top executive coach in Washington, DC, two years running, plus was nominated and selected as a top coach in America by my clients,

- I won two prestigious theater performance roles,

- I've spoken on global stages about leading audaciously, responding instead of reacting to change, and loving who you are, and

- As of publication, I've coached over 350 individuals as they reach up and out to achieve their unique, prismatic, dynamic goals so that they can spread out, get loud, and be boss bitches.

I've looked for ways to grow, fail, rebound, sparkle, and generously share — to give more than I get in a way to leave this world a little bit better than I found it

This forcing yourself into someone else's mode or modality isn't just a personal crisis; it's a global one (and maybe one you've experienced, too?). Across industries, cultures, and communities, people — especially women, women of color, and gender-diverse leaders — are dimming their own brilliance to fit into systems that weren't built for them. The cost? Lost innovation, stifled growth, and a world that keeps spinning on outdated, exclusionary defaults. Imagine if, instead, we all fully stepped into our power — if we collectively decided to take up space, lead audaciously, and stop apologizing for being extraordinary. Workplaces and communities would transform, creativity would explode, and more people would feel seen, valued, and empowered to contribute in ways that actually move the world forward. When we embrace our whole selves, we don't just change our own lives — we create ripple effects that redefine success for everyone. We create a legacy.

This is what I get to do every day as a coach: support glitterbombs as they grab opportunities to discover and amplify the things that make them, them. To choose themselves above everything else. To say Hell Yes. To lead and live with confidence *because of* the things that make them prismatic and unique, not in spite of them.

And most importantly, to feel heard, seen, supported, and supercharged. In doing this work, I've had the sincere pleasure of bringing together some of the brightest and boldest people who seek to do the same for others. To create legacies just by being themselves and, in doing so, giving others permission to be their whole selves, too.

Still, too often those who have big perspectives and bold ideas are told to bottle that up in order to succeed. Quite honestly, that's bullshit.

So, here's what we're going to do together: Throughout these pages, I'm going to equip you with tools to uncover and unleash your truest, most colorful self so that you can stand as an inspiration to others who haven't yet psyched themselves up for their challenges ahead, and to begin to ignite your legacy. Through a sprinkling of science, a few client case studies, and some exercises, you'll own your personal umami-ness and sparkle a little brighter.

Don't worry, it's not as hard as it seems.

Ready? Let's get started.

Here's where you sparkle

At the end of each chapter, I'm offering you an exercise or a resource to build on the stuff I've crammed into these pages. Can you read this book without putting pen-to-paper and finding yourself in the lessons? Sure can, but I invite you to try it anyway.

Coaches aren't consultants: we don't prescribe or dictate the way for you to do things or approach challenges because that solution won't stick. It didn't come from you, so it's not yours. I can share all sorts of information with you, but without spending some time sitting with it, you won't integrate it. You'll understand it—but you won't own it. And owning it? That's where the glitter sticks.

Here's your first chance to find yourself in these pages. Tell me what brought you here. What's your Pinky moment?

_____

_____

_____

_____

_____

_____

_____

1

Given Circumstances

It may come as a surprise to no one and everyone that I was a theater kid. Musicals were a constant on our family turntable, and I spent a good chunk of my elementary school years in drama classes to help me overcome a natural shyness and to channel my creative energy and imagination into play. I had my first professional gig when I was 5, and I was hooked.

I didn't have to worry about feeling awkward or anxious in acting classes or rehearsal rooms because I could escape into a character's skin. I loved telling stories and figuring out how to bring people along with me so that they could feel and experience life outside of their norms — so that maybe, they could also escape for a little while.

Most of all, I loved learning about people and the places that shaped them. I needed to know more about what motivates people, what creates resistance within them, and what makes them who they are at their core. Why do they do what they do when they do? What makes them tick? I quickly became a student of the human condition.

Yep, this former English teacher just cited Wikipedia in her book. My, how the times have changed.

Good ol' Wikipedia defines the human condition as "the characteristics and key events of human life, including birth, learning, emotion, aspiration, reason, morality, conflict, and death" (Human Condition, 2024). Basically, everything that makes you, you, is part of the human condition.

GO ORANGE!

It wasn't until I was in theater school (i.e., college) that I really spent time learning how to study people. Until then and across every professional and extracurricular production I did, I looked for clues in the script, imagined who they were, and went with that. At that time, I didn't research beyond what the text gave me. Many artists don't. Nerdy Virgo artists like adult me do. Both approaches? Perfectly fine.

I'm gonna save you $250k and give you a crash course in conservatory-level Theater 101 — and stick with me here. "Though this be madness, yet there be method in't" (Shakespeare's *Hamlet*, 2.2, ed. 1974).

Around 330 BCE, Aristotle wrote what is believed to be the first treatise on dramatic poetry or dramatic theory, called *Practical Poetics* (Butcher, MacMillan and Co., 1902). *Poetics* is… well, it's about a number of things. But in my education and analysis, it's about how we discharge our lived experiences that we can't otherwise qualify, into art. Any art. And that art becomes a physical representation of what we think and feel, how we behave and interact with people and our environment, and how everything from our past and our present informs our future selves.

Then, sometime in the late-middle of the 19th century, Konstantin Stanislavski took Aristotle's principles and made them actionable and act-able. Those elements of past-self and present-self were retitled to Given Circumstances. To list them out, we have to ask a series of questions:

1. Who am I? — The identity of the character.
2. When am I? — The time period and specific timing within the story.
3. Where am I? — The geographical and physical setting.
4. What do I want? — The reasons behind the character's actions and decisions.
5. Why do I want it? — The underlying motivations driving the character.
6. How will I get it? — The manner in which events unfold, or actions are taken.

From these six questions, generations of artists have built memorable, compelling portrayals of characters that showcase the human condition (New York Film Academy, retrieved 2025).

Actors are obsessed with the human condition. They know that every character — good guy or bad — starts in one place and ends in another. Through their analysis of that character's given circumstances, they're able to parse out goals and objectives in an actionable and enjoyable way.

(End of lecture.)

Stanislavski's six questions aren't just for actors — they're for anyone who wants to own their story, reclaim their choices, and own the main character energy of their own life. Right now, in this moment, the six questions matter because too many of us are living by someone else's script, making decisions based on external expectations, fears, or past conditioning rather than what we actually want.

You answer these questions every day. We all do, regardless of which stage we find ourselves on or what story we're telling about ourselves at that time. Every day, you unconsciously take stock of all of the experiences that have gotten you to this moment to help choose your next move. YOUR next move, not something someone else wants for you.

- Because it's all about choice — choosing your adventure so that you can:
- Believe you deserve the change you're working for
- Say yes to something new
- Break old habits and try on fresh ones
- Align your heart, your mind, and your soul so that you're not battling against yourself
- Unapologetically, unashamedly want something that's only for you

In August 2020, I had the opportunity to attend a webinar led by Dr. Dana Sims, "The Business Case for a Radical Sabbatical." *Check her* Dr. Sims led attendees first through the journey of buying a sailboat *out at:* and living on it with her partner and their menagerie. The webinar *fedability.com* then took attendees through a process applicable to making Big Moves; it offered attendees a chance to be both rad and radical.

At its core, Dr. Sims' webinar offered a casual-but-huge takeaway about mitigating uncertainties at decision points: Choose Yourself.

Yes, assess the benefits and the risks, the costs and consequences, but choose yourself in the end. Those two simple words have stuck with me for years now, at the front of my mind and on the tip of my tongue.

Of course I choose me, don't I? Sure. Yes. Mostly. Often. The more I thought about choosing myself, the more my certainty about actually doing it faltered.

I chose the college I attended because they gave me the most financial aid to support the field I decided to study, and that was the field I chose because my college counselor suggested I wouldn't get into other programs of study. Financial aid plus adult guidance does not equal choosing me.

I stayed at jobs where I was harassed or devalued for way too long because I didn't want to disappoint the very people who were harassing and devaluing me... Choosing pain and discomfort does not equal choosing me.

I wanted to be a writer. Funny how things work out in the end.

I once got a tattoo that was larger, darker and literally not what I wanted because it was what my partner at the time wanted... Not. Choosing. Me.

This not-choosing-me mental list reflected patterns in my thought processes and behaviors; reasons and excuses and external factors that I allowed to influence decisions that I made not necessarily for my own benefit, but to prevent the discomfort or disappointment of others.

Hands up if you're also a people pleaser?

A second list, choosing-only-for-me, bubbled up radiant moments when I let go of what I thought or imagined were exterior expectations and said yes to my instincts, my needs and my wants:

- I left an unhealthy marriage because I woke up one morning and realized that the weight of that life wasn't sustainable; that that couldn't be it for me.

- I bought a Mini Cooper because I wanted to, and it supported my commuting needs, and it reduced my fuel and car payment expenses; plus, I looked really damn cute driving it.

- I allowed friendships to fall away because we weren't helping each other be our best selves, because things had become one-sided, or because I didn't like who I was with those people.
- I took a leap to open a business during a global pandemic because I wanted to work differently, I wanted my days to have new meaning, and I wanted the hustle to be for me.

Those moments of choosing myself have led to little joys, greater happiness and more opportunities to thrive. I choose myself because I deserve to after years of not living for me.

So do you.

And here's the big, shiny truth: understanding your given circumstances—the raw, real, sometimes messy facts of who you are and where you've been—is what clears the stage for you to *choose yourself* again and again. You can't own your story if you're still trapped in someone else's version of you. Getting clear about your life, your dreams, your motivations? It's your neon-lit off-ramp to living electrically, audaciously, and vividly. No edits. No dimming. Just full-throttle, spotlight-on, glitter-everywhere YOU.

I spend gads of time with clients unpacking why they can't do things.

"They expect something else from me."

"What if I disappoint them?"

"I don't want to seem selfish!"

All valid, selfless reasons to avoid social discomfort. And when we talk about the cost of those decisions, I always, always think about Dr. Sims' life on the high seas and ask "What happens if you choose yourself?"

When you get clear on your own Given Circumstances — the who, what, when, where, why, and how that make you *you* — you don't have to audition for your own life anymore. Choose it. Own it.

Curtain's up, glitterbomb. It's showtime.

✳✳✳

Here's where you sparkle

In order to know where you're going, you need to have a solid idea of where you are and how you got here. Here's what I'd like you to do.

Grab a piece of paper, open a blank document on your laptop, however it feels right for you.

I want you to draw a little graph, or use this one:

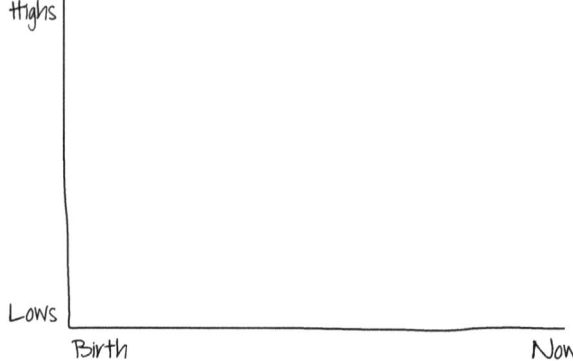

On that graph and starting from birth, capture the milestones and defining moments. The highs and lows. When you're done, connect the dots, like this:

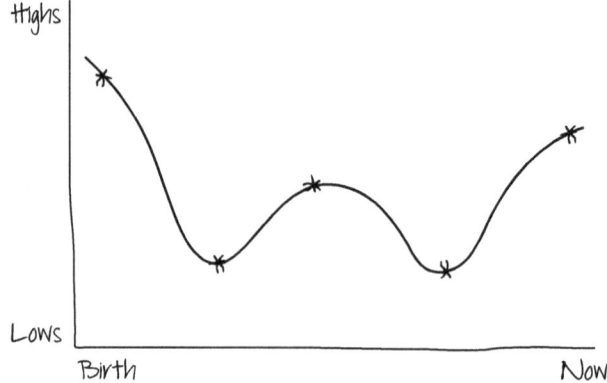

You can even label those points so that future-you doesn't forget what present-you captured.

And now using Stanislavski's questions, introduce yourself to me with a clear understanding of before and now.

Who are you? _____

_____

_____

_____

_____

When are you? _____

_____

_____

_____

_____

Where are you? _____

_____

_____

_____

_____

What do you want? _____

_____

_____

_____

_____

Why do you want it? _____

_____

_____

_____

_____

How are you gonna get it? _____

_____

_____

_____

_____

2

Owning What I Want

Before we can even glimmer-in-your-eye about legacy, we need to be super clear about your 'I Want' Statement.

<claps hands> PLACES EVERYONE.

As you learned from the last chapter, my background is in theater, specifically musical theater. There's this moment that happens in the first 15 minutes of a musical, when the main character sings a big, soaring song that expresses an emotion or a desire or a need or a want for themselves. This is the main character's goal, and it's what the entire musical is going to be about. It's a moment of reflection and longing. It's a pause in the action that immediately accelerates the plot. And it's called an 'I Want' song.

Is there an 'I want' song that comes to mind for you?

It is because of my musical theater nerdiness that I refer to goals as 'I Want' statements. 'I Want' builds on your given circumstances (remember chapter 1?). Without knowing what you want, you're going to flounder around. It's going to be really unsatisfying and confusing — you'll feel like you're not making any progress.

You deserve to harness this main character energy and be the protagonist of your own life. Proudly proclaiming what you want not only allows you to step into the spotlight and turn up the volume on your truest, most colorful self, but it also helps you

If musical theater isn't your jam, this also applies to any Disney movie that includes singing.

80% of the time when I ask this question, people respond "I want to be where the people are!" from The Little Mermaid or "How Far I'll Go" from Moana. Sometimes, I get "My Shot" from Hamilton, or "The Wizard and I" from Wicked.

move beyond your internal clusterfuck and get clear on what you're actually working so hard for.

Your 'I Want' statement reflects something that doesn't currently exist in your life. For whatever reason, and I cannot explain it, an 'I Want' statement is really hard to own. It's just two simple little words: I. Want. Maybe it's because it involves standing with confidence, self-assurance, and a little bit of healthy ego, and proclaiming something for yourself? Your 'I Want' is beautiful and complicated and scary, and a commitment to you and only you. It's going to make you feel vulnerable. But I promise you, proclaiming it is absolutely worth it because the rewards are tremendous.

First, let's remember your given circumstances. If you need a prompt, try reflecting on where you are with one of these:

- Your career
- Your free time
- Your well-being
- Your finances
- Your physical environment
- Your relationships

Whatever element of your life is important for you to focus on you right now.

Next, imagine where you want to be in that element. Does that thought make your toes tingle with excitement? Does it also make you want to puke?

If the answer to both of those questions is yes, then HELL YES.

If it's not, can you go one step further? How about getting more specific? Be as bold as you're feeling brave enough to be. Release your inner badass.

Sometimes we stop ourselves from dreaming big. We hesitate to own what we actually want. We wonder "but what if I can't have what I want?"

I promise you: your dream is not too big. Knowing what you want is the first step to turning 'I Want' into 'I Am.' It clarifies what it is that you're working so hard for. With that clarity, your next move will come into focus, and you'll see actionable, tangible opportunities to make changes for yourself.

Thinking about your goals as 'I Wants' changes your framing because there's no right or wrong way to want things. 'I Want' gets you to think about trying things out for yourself without the fear of failing. It gets you away from right/wrong and into The Funknown™.

You're not misreading: I am writing the words 'fun' and 'known' together — The Funknown™.

The Funknown™ is the in-between. It is the space that occupies the no-gal's-land between where you are today (the as-is) and where you want to be (I want). It's a place of exploration, of play and of discovery where there's no one way of doing things — only opportunity. It's the place where you're becoming your fullest self.

Is the phrase a little cutesy? Sure. But so are you. So cute. We're gonna talk a lot more about this later.

In The Funknown™ we exuberantly own what we want for ourselves.

With the day-to-day hustle, it can be tough to find time to pull back, breathe and reflect on whether or not this is what you really want. But when you do, something vibrantly unexpected happens.

Take my client, Raya. Raya had always been a high producer, high performer, and high achiever — the kind of person whose career was always trending upward. They worked long, demanding days before returning home to their young family. Yes, they were exhausted and carried the constant weight of parent-guilt. But providing for their family was something they were deeply proud of.

Real quick note here: when I talk about my clients in these pages, I'm using pseudonyms.

In 2023, they had a once-in-a-lifetime work opportunity present itself: an invitation to level up in a way they'd never dreamed and have more visibility and a great impact to their field and community. It would mean longer hours, steeper sacrifices, and less time at home. But it would only be four years. And hey — they could do anything for four years.

Raya had been looking for opportunities to make the right change.

They were itchy to try something new. They would have preferred a bit more work/life integration, but this opportunity felt like something they couldn't pass up.

They hesitated about this offer. It didn't feel right. It didn't feel good. But it was a logical extension of their hard work and career goals, but when they really tuned in to it, the offer felt like standing at the foot of yet another mountain that looked just like the last six they had already climbed. No real growth. No real joy. Just... inertia dressed up as in a shiny, new outfit.

The easy, expected thing would have been to accept the position and not think twice about it. But the easy thing and the right thing are so often not the same.

Maybe read that again and give it a highlight.

So, Raya took a moment and asked "What am I working so hard for when I can't enjoy the things that hard work brings for my family? Is this what I really, truly, honestly want?"

Raya found themselves living for a life they weren't actually part of. That reflection cracked something open in them.

They didn't accept the position.

Instead, they left their job in order to be a full-time parent for a while. During that time, they got clear on what they wanted their life and career to actually feel like, not just look like. They focused on aligning their values with the things they wanted for themselves and their family. They kicked expectations in the face.

The biggest surprise? They didn't miss the rush, the deadlines, the constant emails. They missed themselves. In the quiet, they found tiny rebellions — midday walks, restarting something from their cemetery of half-started hobbies, reading a whole book for pleasure — and they realized that joy isn't in the hustle; it's in the everyday.

They stopped climbing mountains that weren't meant for them.

I know this type of option—ostensibly blowing up your professional life— isn't available to everyone. Raya needed to make this change in order to choose themselves and have the time and space to focus, BUT there is an option for you in the spirit of this decision.

Raya's story reminds us not to choose what's expected just because it's expected. Don't choose what you think they want you to do.

Choose adventure.

Choose what inspires you.

Choose what you want.

And if you feel like you need permission to be bold, specific, brave, and selfish: here it is. PERMISSION GRANTED.

Here's where you sparkle

We've been talking about the power of 'I Want' to help you clarify where you're going while owning and honoring your whole self.

Let's take our last moments together in this chapter and make your 'I Wants' actionable.

That's the trickiest part, isn't it? How often have you set a goal for yourself, been super psyched about it, and then gotten nowhere because you lost steam/ didn't know where to start/misplaced your accountability/made excuses?

I get it. Me too.

STEP 1

If you haven't already, write down your 'I Want' statement:

_____

_____

_____

_____

_____

_____

_____

Then, take a moment to look at it. REALLY look at it.

What does success actually look like when you've turned your 'I Want' into 'I Am'? While we're at it, what does it smell like, taste like, and sound like?

_____

_____

_____

_____

_____

_____

Imagine that moment you've turned your 'I Want' into 'I Am'.

What will you be doing differently in your life/business/career when you've achieved your goal?

_____

_____

_____

_____

_____

_____

Based on the answers to these questions, do you want or need to revise your 'I Want?'

_____

_____

_____

_____

_____

_____

_____

STEP 2

Break that big I Want into little, bite-sized pieces. What are three things that you can do to kickstart your journey from 'I Want' to 'I Am'?

Think about it like this: In order to {'I WANT'}, I will {ONE IDEA}, {SECOND IDEA}, and {THIRD IDEA}.

In order to _____,

I will _____,

_____,

and_____.

Remember: these ideas are intended to come from a place of play and experimentation. No one is going to grade this work. No one but you even needs to see it.

STEP 3

Now, I'm going to ask you three questions that my clients always, always get annoyed at me for bringing up. They're not trick questions, I promise.

In Step 1, you identified how success appears to your senses. These questions force you to quantify the qualitative:

By what date will you try to act on those three ideas?

_____

How will you measure your progress?

_____

_____

_____

_____

How will you stay accountable to your goals? Do you want an accountabilibuddy?

_____

_____

_____

_____

Now, get to work. And let me know how it's going!

3

Into The Funknown™

So often when we think about crafting our 'I Wants,' there's a feeling that there's a right way and a wrong way to do things, *and* we're encouraged to be very focused on the end result. I disagree. When we spend too much time chasing "what's expected" or "what's right," we miss the opportunity to bring ourselves to the party. That's where creativity is: in disrupting the expected, the traditional, the accepted by infusing the things that make you, you. You are dynamic and luminescent. Enjoy exploring what happens when you amplify those qualities instead of hiding them.

That space in between where you are and where you want to be is a place of becoming. It's the messy middle. It's a place of play and discovery and curiosity. As I mentioned earlier, I call it The Funknown™.

When people don't know what they're coming up against, they become anxious. Change is a stressor and people have been preconditioned to believe that change has to be hard. This is an attempt to flip the script. In The Funknown™, there's no one way of doing things — there's no right or wrong. Only opportunity. It's an opening to allow people into the process of becoming what's on the other side. It isn't about free-falling into chaos. It's about stepping into the space where possibility lives. It's where creativity, curiosity, and reinvention thrive. It's where we shed the "shoulds" and play with the "what ifs."

Angellika was restless.

From the outside, everything looked fine. Great, even. Every day felt like clockwork. Up early. Coffee. Commute. Back-to-back meetings. A neatly packed lunch eaten at her desk. She kept her social circle tidy and her romantic life sensible. Predictable routines, and a life that was, by all accounts, successful. But inside? She felt like she was living in beige. Like she had lost her sparkle somewhere between back-to-back meetings, the expectations of everyone around her, and the safe, responsible choices she had been making for years.

"I feel like I lost my mojo," she told me in our intro chat. "I used to be so full of ideas, energy, and adventure. Now? I just... go through the motions."

She wasn't unhappy, exactly. But she wasn't excited either. And that, to her, was worse.

Angellika was standing at the edge of The Funknown™ — that space between who she was and who she wanted to be. She felt like she was on the edge of change, staring into the abyss.

So, we started with an experiment. Instead of trying to force clarity — because forcing never works — we embraced curiosity. We made space for play. I challenged Angellika to pick one thing she'd always wanted to try but never had. Not because it was logical. Not because it would lead to something concrete. Just because it lit her up.

She chose flying trapeze.

It had been years since she let herself be ridiculous. To be in the moment without a plan. And let me tell you, the first class? Absolute disaster. She panicked. Overthought everything. Wanted to quit. But she kept showing up. And something shifted. She started laughing — really laughing — for the first time in a long time. She got comfortable with not knowing what came next. She built new physical and mental muscles for the mind-over-matter experience of letting go, and those muscles didn't just show up under the tent. They started showing up in her work. In her relationships. In the way she tackled decisions and opportunities. The "breakthrough" wasn't a single lightbulb moment — it was a slow build, starting with playful experimentation.

Then came the big shift. One day, after months of playing in The Funknown™, she realized she was no longer scared of uncertainty — she was excited by it. She was trying new things at work, shaking up her routine, saying yes to things before she had all the answers. She wasn't waiting for excitement to find her. She was creating it.

Angellika didn't need to throw her whole life away to feel alive again. She needed to trust herself enough to step into The Funknown™ — to make space for curiosity, play, and risk without demanding guarantees. And in doing that, she found the thing she thought she'd lost forever: her mojo.

Her next "pick one thing"? A cross-country move. Just her, her cat, and a wide-open sense of possibility. Her job was portable. "For the first time in years," she told me, "I have no idea what's coming next. And I've never been more excited."

When you're looking at your life and you're putting goals into place…

When you're weighing whether to choose this thing over that thing…

When you're figuring out what's a yes and what's a no…

That's The Funknown™ at work, my friend. And if you're ready to play in that space, I promise — mojo is waiting for you too.

It's not always obvious what to choose. It's not always easy to choose, either. Fear is very real. And it can derail your exploration and discovery.

The thing is, embracing uncertainty can release your need for control, reduce stress and anxiety, and lead to increased resilience and adaptability. An openness to uncertainty fosters a growth mindset, encouraging exploration beyond your comfort zone and facilitating the discovery of one's true self (Whiting, 2024). Becoming comfortable with uncertainty enhances creativity and divergent thinking, leading to novel ideas and solutions. Like Angellika, you leap, and the trapeze bar will appear.

There's a moment that happens during a coaching engagement that has become predictable, right around our seventh session together. We're beyond those initial, invigorating conversations during which we're defining your 'I Want' and really imagining what it looks and feels and tastes like, and starting to get really specific about what it will take to make that 'I Want' into an 'I Am'. You're smack in the middle of moving towards your goal. You're

We've already started to do this in the "Here's where you sparkle" section of chapter 2! Look at you: getting a head start!

embracing new behaviors and approaches, and you're exploring The Funknown™. You can see your 'I Want' — you can alllllmost touch it.

Things. Are. Happening.

And then your Imposter Inner Voice (your IIV) shows up and throws some cold water on your spark. Your confidence dramatically plummets. Your progress stops. And then you arrive to our coaching session and ask: What if I can't reach my goal?

This "what if I can't" moment isn't actually about doubting your abilities. It's not. Your IIV wouldn't have popped into view if your goals were too far-fetched. It's why I invite you to select 'I Wants' that make your toes tingle and make you want to puke: the bigger your emotional response to your 'I Wants,' the more likely you are to worker harder for them because they're real to you.

We have a whole chapter coming up about your Imposter Inner Voice, i.e. Imposter Syndrome. I couldn't call myself a coach without including one.

No, this moment of doubt is purely about loving yourself. It's about balancing the fear of failure against the fear of succeeding and deciding how much risk you're willing to accept in order to move forward. Both are at play. Fear of failure offers the self-sabotage of anxiety about negative outcomes, loss, or judgement. Fear of succeeding focuses on concerns about new expectations, a change in identity, worrying you're going to become the target of external criticism — these are the intrusive thoughts that typically come in loudly with "I don't deserve this."

The key difference is that fear of failure focuses on the pain of loss/rejection, while fear of success centers on the newness about handling positive changes and their outcomes.

We stumble through this moment of doubt together. To protect your squishy nougat center. To reset and re-calibrate. To revisit what brought you to coaching in the first place. To celebrate the distance you've traveled and the opportunities to come. To know your limits

My heart hurts every single time I'm asked this question. And we're gonna talk about this more in the next chapter, k?

and back-up plans and not actually need them, because you've allowed yourself the fear but didn't allow yourself to be stymied by it.

And the one question you can sure as shit expect I'm going to ask you, "What will it take for you to go love yourself?"

To do like Angellika, embrace The Funknown™, and get your mojo back?

Because friend, you goddamn deserve to.

The outcome may not be what you thought it would, but that's because you've allowed yourself the adventure along the way. You reveled in The Funknown™.

***
Here's where you sparkle

When we're talking about facing our fear of failure and/or success, we're also talking about taking calculated risks that require balancing rewards against potential downsides. The key is to take action and make moves while maintaining the ability to bounce back and try again. To build confidence and capability little by little.

And in order to do this, we're going to do one of my favorite activities: Catastrophizing. But we're not going to get stuck there, glitterbomb. We're not trauma rolling in the negative what-could-be's. We're going to allow ourselves the negative so that we can rebound faster if we need to.

Take a look at your 'I Want' Statement.

Set a timer for 3 minutes, and imagine what might get in the way of achieving this goal? Write it down or type it out — get it out of your head.

1. _____

2. _____

3. _____

4. _____

5. _____

6. _____

7. _____

8. _____

9. _____

10. _____

Now, reset that timer for 3 minutes and, for each get-in-the-wayer, think about one way you can prevent or mitigate that obstacle. Flip the negative to a positive.

1. _____

2. _____

3. _____

4. _____

5. _____

6. _____

7. _____

8. _____

9. _____

10. _____

Reset that timer for 3 minutes one last time. What scares you about achieving this goal? Get it out of your IIV's catalog.

_____

_____

_____

_____

_____

_____

_____

Now, for each fear, write an "I deserve" statement.

_____

_____

_____

_____

_____

_____

_____

For example, if my fear is "I might lose a long-term acquaintance by drawing new boundaries with my time," my statement would be "I deserve to have people in my life who respect the boundaries I place, because I respect theirs in return."

Read those "I deserves" out loud. Yes. Out loud.

We're aiming for practice, not perfection. For play and reflection and discovery, not "expertise." When you hear yourself own what you deserve, you start to believe it little by little. It opens new neural pathways for opportunity and exploration.

Welcome to The Funknown™.

4

The "But-What-If" Mixtape

If we spoke about generations like we do our zodiac signs, then I'd be an Elder Millennial with Gen X rising. The music of my teenage angst informed how I dressed and what clique I found myself in at school. For better or worse, those songs still hit me in my formative-years-feels.

I can still remember what songs I thoughtfully, obsessively curated for (first) mixtapes and (later) mix-CDs, and what song was my signature bonus track selection regardless of the message I intended to convey with each mixtape. They were a mix of tracks pulled from cassettes, vinyl, and radio, and ranged from Madonna (always) to Neil Diamond, to Alanis and Nirvana, to the Spice Girls and Disney's *Aladdin* soundtrack or *The Phantom Of The Opera* London cast album. Sometimes there were commercials from the radio that may have been inside jokes. Sometimes I read a poem. Yep.

These 75-minute cassette tapes were love letters. Platonic. Crush-thirsty. Penitent. Vengeful. Earnest and vulnerable and cringey and funny. I found a stack of them in the attic when my mom downsized from our childhood home. While I don't have a way to play them, I'm holding onto them like the precious artform they are. My partner also made me two mix-CDs when we were dating, and while I have the songs themselves in a playlist on my phone, the physical CD and liner notes are framed and hanging on the wall in our bedroom.

It's Mariah Carey's "All I Want For Christmas Is You," which was first released in October 1994. That song is a bop in June and December.

Those songs play on a loop in my head. I am the type of person who will quote — or more likely, erupt into — song when it fits the conversation. My inner world is musical. Because of this musicality, there are elements of adult life that play out in my head like the mixtapes of my youth.

In 1978, Pauline Rose Clance and Susanne Imes wrote a paper that introduced the term Imposter Phenomenon to the world. Imposter Phenomenon "designate[s] an internal experience of intellectual phonies, which appears to be particularly prevalent and intense among a select sample of high achieving women" (Clance, retrieved 2025).

Those experiencing this phenomenon, say Clance and Imes, persist "in believing that they [high-achieving women] are really not bright and have fooled anyone who thinks otherwise. Numerous achievements, which one might expect to provide ample objective evidence of superior intellectual functioning, do not appear to affect the impostor belief." They also wrote a handy quiz to accompany the paper, helping quizzers determine how much the phenomenon interferes with their lives. I'm not including that here because I don't want to cause you any more stress than you already have; and honestly, you don't need that confirmation bias.

Anyway.

You've heard of her sisters, right? Imposter Syndrome and Imposter Complex?

Women are more likely to experience Imposter Phenomenon than their male counterparts, although men may also experience this doubt and uncertainty. I spend a lot of time talking with clients who have this Imposter Inner Voice (IIV) as a secondary soundtrack running through their minds, and it's not only about business.

These are just a few examples I've heard from my clients. The IIV critiques your:

Relationships: making it hard to really say what you feel, or maybe unintentionally you take things out of context, or you don't feel like you deserve someone's attention, time, or love.

Parenting skills: making you feel like you're not good enough, you're letting your kids down, or you're comparing yourself to other parents.

Work: making you doubt your credibility, your value, or your impact. It may also make you think you don't deserve the seat at the table that you've worked so hard for.

You name it, your IIV has something to say about it.

Here's when it's likely to speak up: when you're pushing against your comfort zone. When you find yourself trying something new or stretching your potential, your IIV is going to speak up and assist you in retreating to your comfort zone by introducing self-sabotaging thoughts, or what I like to call the But-What-If Mixtape. It's the greatest hits of your insecurities stacked to have the maximum impact on your ego and your soul. It's a self-defense mechanism that hinders growth. An anti-love note to yourself.

The passion and intention that go into making a mixtape for someone — a carefully curated journey of emotion, storytelling, and connection — are the same forces that fuel the But-What-If Mixtape. The difference? One is created from love and the other from self-sabotage. Just like every mixtape tells a story, our insecurities and doubts stack up in a way that feels personal, intimate, and inescapable. Those thoughts can keep stacking up the more you think about them. They become familiar, like an album you know track-by-track. But here's the thing: just like we can create a playlist that lifts us up, we can rewrite the But-What-If track list to work *for us* instead of against us.

What's very important to remember is that, at some point, everyone will doubt their experiences, accomplishments, and skills. Everyone doubts themselves. It's common. Honest.

If you read about imposter phenomenon, you'll see suggestions about shaking off perfectionism, finding a support system to lift you out of the doubt, and recognizing the IIV when it happens, owning your agency and defining a pathway through the doubt.

Here's what I'd like to add into the mix: pre-empt the But-What-If .

You know the hooks and the themes and the feelings that your IIV will elicit. Give yourself the space to disaster plan the But-What-Ifs before they even pop into your head. If you're going to have those intrusive thoughts anyway, why not put them to work to reward your future self? Here's an example of what I mean:

> *Thought:* But-What-If I show up for this meeting and I'm not able to participate meaningfully because I'm not an expert in the topic?

Ask: How Might I prepare for the meeting in order to feel safe participating from a place of curiosity and growth?

Option: I'll explore the agenda, try to sync up with someone more knowledgeable in advance, or prep a couple of questions to bring into the conversation that acknowledge my desire to learn and understand.

Thought: But-What-If my audition was a fluke and they discover I'm not as talented as they originally thought when they offered me this role?

Ask: How Might I feel more confident in stepping into the rehearsal room and seeking out the feedback I need in order to believe I'm making expected progress?

Option: I'll do as much pre-production research as I can. I'll have character-driven choices prepared but be willing to accept adjustments. I'll know my character's given circumstances cold. I'll ask for clarification. I'll welcome notes from the director, and I'll also ask for notes or specific feedback on scenes where I'm feeling less secure.

Imposter syndrome, self-doubt, and fear of failure are baked into the cultural narratives you've been fed. You've been conditioned to question your worth, shrink your ambitions, and second-guess your achievements. The world loses out when brilliant, capable people like you hold back from stepping into leadership, pursuing bold ideas, or even just owning your damn space.

Imagine what could change — what innovation, what equity, what radical, effervescent joy could exist — if we all stopped believing the But-What-Ifs and started choosing ourselves instead.

The first step? Answering those But-What-Ifs for yourself during your moments of strength and confidence so that when doubt creeps in, your badass self has already prepped you to brush the IIV to the side. Plus, this little bit of preparation will help prevent you from unspooling in those moments of doubt and discomfort.

I invite you into my swagger. I'm not an imposter. I'm a goddamn phenomenon.

And so are you. ⟶ Wanna read more on this subject? Of the 5 million Google hits you get on this topic, I return to the Harvard Business Review article, "Stop Telling Women They Have Imposter Syndrome," by Ruchika Tulshyan and Jodi-Ann Burey

Here's where you sparkle

Alright friend. It's time to write out the track list for your But-What-If mixtape. Really, get it out of your head. Even just saying it out loud will make it feel less big and scary. Think of this as self-care. Let present-you take care of future-you.

Beside each T (for Thought,) write out a track title. This can be a title you make up, or an actual song that applies to your thoughts. Then, complete the A (Ask) and O (Option) for each.

T _____

    A _____

    O _____

T _____

    A _____

    O _____

T _____

    A _____

    O _____

T _____

  A_____

    O _____

T _____

  A_____

    O _____

T _____

  A_____

    O _____

T _____

  A_____

    O _____

T _____

  A_____

    O _____

T _____

A _____

O _____

T _____

A _____

O _____

WANNA SPARKLE MORE? Create an actual pump-you-up playlist of songs to get you out of your head and into your power and play it loudly on those days when you need a little pick-me-up. Need some inspiration? Check out Uproar Coaching's community playlist. Scan the QR code below. Add to it. Take from it. Rock out with your bad self.

5

Your Truest, Most Colorful Self

When I attended my first coaching training intensive, an early homework assignment we were given was to ask people who are close to us to describe us using three words. Whoever I asked would not be permitted to explain why they selected the words they did, and I wasn't permitted to ask.

I procrastinated this assignment for much longer than I'd like to admit, out of fear of the vulnerable place I'd be in as recipient of the words. The teen version of me still occasionally crowds my heart with the emotional turmoil of adolescent taunts and trauma. Ghosts of negative reviews from my time onstage haunt my dreams. Professional put-downs from back-handed compliments over a decade ago still sting. I know what people have said to me; about me.

The more confident you appear, the more the world tries to chip away at you. The more yourself you try to be, the more you're othered and expected to change. It's a strange social paradox called Tall Poppy Syndrome (Women of Influence, retrieved 2025), when the more confident and authentic you are, the more you can become a target for those who feel threatened, uncomfortable, or challenged by your presence. The tallest poppy gets cut down to ensure that it does not outshine or overshadow the rest.

This is the only place where "it's not you, it's me" applies.

Here's how I consistently described myself at the time I was given this assignment, without explanation or disclaiming:

Difficult
Overachiever
No-nonsense
Strange
Clever

I looked at that list, and I thought: those are powerful words, but they're not necessarily kind words. Can I over-explain my reasons for choosing those words? Sure, but who really gives a damn? The point is, the way I talk about myself is fueled from a lifetime of allowing other people into my head to define me, for me.

The way we describe ourselves is powerful as hell. It's like holding up a mirror, except the reflection is a funhouse distortion shaped by other people's opinions, old narratives we've absorbed, and whatever mood our IIV is in that day. Social psychologist Charles Horton Cooley called this the looking-glass self — the idea that we shape our identities based on how we think others see us (Cooley, 1922). Meaning? The words we choose to describe ourselves aren't just words — they become the scaffolding for how we move through the world. If you keep calling yourself "difficult," you'll start to carry that weight. If you start saying "direct" instead, you'll stand a little taller in that truth. That's why this three-word exercise is more than just a feel-good assignment; it's a reclamation.

While I kind of cheated on my coaching homework — I'll explain this in a moment — I gave myself a secondary assignment: make my personal descriptors shinier and more of a reflection of the beautiful mermaid that I want to know I am.

And so:

Difficult → Direct
Overachiever → Prepared
No-nonsense → Straightforward
Strange → Unconventional
Clever → Brilliant

Literally reading those back to myself now to check my spelling is like releasing a held breath. I feel better. Both sets of words are accurate descriptions of who I am and what I put out into the world. They're honest. ⟶

However you choose to label it, being genuine, real, and true to yourself is in that beautiful Venn diagram intersection of your internal values, beliefs, and feelings, and your external behaviors and actions (Davis, 2021). As you know, Glitterbomb, 'being all of you' — or as much of you as you feel safe being in whatever environment you're in and how much of you they deserve — often requires courage because it may involve going against the grain, standing up for your beliefs, and risking disapproval or rejection from others. Having confidence in your truest, most colorful self will give you the courage to take these risks in order to remain true to who you are. And who you are is so important. Let's not compromise that.

So, back to my homework and how I cheated. I asked my nieces and nephews, then all under the age of 7, for three words they'd use to describe me. I figured I could more easily laugh away their responses if I needed to. I also asked my partner. Removing duplicates, here's the list they came up with:

Patient	Kind
Silly	Nice
Adventurer	Goofy
Colorful	Brave
Unexpected	Cozy

There's no reason to laugh those words away. They're not wrong.

All these iterations of the Three Word Exercise aren't just a reflection — they're a reclamation. They're breadcrumbs leading you back to your most prismatic, unapologetic self.

Because everything you've done so far — owning your Given Circumstances, naming your 'I Want,' playing in The Funknown™, unwinding your But-What-If mixtape — has been leading to

Look, I'd add the word "Authentic" to the end of this sentence, but it's a word that's become wildly overused and co-opted within the last five years, and its meaning has become diluted, and it's a word I really dislike. Originally intended to signify truth and integrity, it's been weaponized by social media and marketing professionals as a buzzword. It's performative. No thank you.

this: a chance to unclusterfuck your identity. To cut the strings of who you were told to be and name who you actually are. The words you choose to describe yourself aren't just a vibe. They're your glitterbomb manifesto. No more shrinking to fit a role you never auditioned for. This is your callback for the part of a lifetime: the truest, most colorful version of you.

This is proof: You are seen. You are necessary. And the world is infinitely better because you exist in it, just as you are.

Here's where you sparkle

We're gonna do this 3-word exercise, through all of the iterations I talked through above. Ready?

STEP 1

Jot down 3-5 words you'd use to describe yourself. Don't overthink and try not to disclaim/explain.

1. _____

2. _____

3. _____

STEP 2

Reclaim your headspace and let these words shine. Take a breath and give yourself a break by drawing a line from the original 3 words to something potentially more positive.

Were you positive right out of the gate? Hell yes glitterbomb! Skip to Step 3.

1. _____

2. _____

3. _____

STEP 3

Ask those you love to describe you in 3 words, without explanation. Capture their words in a running list, grouping "like" words with each other.

1. _____

2. _____

3. _____

4. _____

5. _____

6. _____

7. _____

8. _____

9. _____

10. _____

STEP 4

Compare your 3 words with the list from loved ones (draw little arrows, if you want). Where is there overlap? What do you put out into the world that other people witness and feel, that maybe you've overlooked in yourself? What surprises you? What feels right?

_____

_____

_____

_____

_____

_____

_____

_____

Keep both lists within reach, particularly on a rainy day. Being your truest, most colorful self is hard. Not compromising who you are based on the expectations of others is really hard. When you're feeling yourself bending into molds that aren't honest to who you are, grab your list and remind yourself of your dynamic and prismatic glow.

6

Too Much?

It feels like a million years ago at this point, but when my partner and I were dating he was in a performance that required him to wear extensive amounts of gold body glitter. Whenever I saw him during the run of that show, he left a trail of glitter behind him even when it had been several days and several more showers since he was onstage. I found it on couch cushions and between floorboards. On my cat Athena's tail. On a cup that had gone through the dishwasher. It was literally everywhere, and it somehow followed us when we moved in together and then bought a house several years later.

Now, I love glitter for its stick-aroundness. I taught my very young nieces and nephews to rub sparkly cards or holiday ornaments on their hands and then their arms or clothes. Yes, it's terrible of me. But it's also a lot of fun to see how those early (bad) habits have stuck around as they enter double-digits. I've heard glitter referred to as the herpes of crafting supplies, and it's true. That stuff will stick to you forever, lying in wait until the moment you least expect it.

I also love glitter for its festivity. Even a single flake on someone's face feels joyful. Plus, you know something extra is about to happen when there's glitter associated with it. Whatever it is deserves a bit more flash and flair.

I am a lot, Glitterbomb.

I'm a lot of look. I'm a lot of energy. I'm a lot of volume. I effervesce and I luminesce, and I stand out. I have Opinions.

Yes, I understand when I need to read the room and adjust, but I'm never not all of me. For many, many reasons it took me a long time to become comfortable in the hum of my own skin, to feel the pride-of-being-me, and so I refuse to not be a true version of myself, even if at library-hush volume.

The world often asks me to not be me. My clients also hear the same "constructive feedback" on ways to embrace sameness. We've been called "too much," and not in an affectionate way.

Too much means "understand your place."

Too much means "be smaller."

Too much means "act more like how people in this situation have traditionally acted."

Too much means othering.

In the first pages of this book, I introduced you to Business Kari. Remember her? She dressed and styled in a certain way. She wasn't overly showy with piercings or makeup or jewelry. She even had a business voice and a business presence.

As you know from earlier in this book, both Business Kari and IRL Kari were miserable. I was miserable because I was boxing myself in: my approach to work, my way of leading, and how I represented myself in the world in a way that was completely dishonest to who I truly was at my core. I actively toned down my colorfulness to fit in.

Through the years, I have seen other unconventional doers and dreamers become more beige with each passing day. Our presence, voices, and expertise have been diminished because we approach things in a new and different way. We're a threat to "the way it's always been done."

And it's a shame. It's a shame because these people are necessary — the unusual and unexpected people who stick with us after our time with them has ended. They're the glitter that lingers long after the card has been recycled, or the body makeup has been washed away.

Society loves to put people into neat little boxes with labels like "approachable", "team player", or "good culture fit". But the second you bring a little presence into the room — speak up, take space, own your expertise — the tone shifts. Suddenly, you're "too much." Too bold, too opinionated, too ambitious, too something. Research backs this up: women displaying leadership behaviors

— the exact ones that get men promoted, by the way — are more likely to be judged as aggressive, difficult, or even unlikable (WOI Editorial Team, 2024). The same presence that makes you a force gets recast as a liability when you don't shrink to fit outdated expectations. Workplace culture doesn't just reflect these biases — it reinforces them. (Stamarski and Son Hing, 2015) And let's be real: that kind of exhausting social tightrope walk keeps brilliant, capable people from stepping fully into their power.

But here's the truth — your presence is not the problem. The problem is a system that wasn't built to hold this much brilliance. So, the choice isn't whether or not you're "too much." The choice is whether you keep trying to fit into a space that was never designed for you — or you own the fact that you deserve better. Different.

The next time someone says you're too much, ask them two questions:

1. Too much for whom? This will generally be met with an awkward pause and a nervous pivot — stay with them and ask again, respectfully.

2. What is it that you think I should be doing differently? My favorite response to this question — and the one I've heard most frequently is — "Well, if I was in your situation, I would do…" which welcomes a lovely conversation about the value in differences of perspective, experiences, and approaches. Also, it's their opinion and not actionable feedback. So do with that what you will.

Or don't. Accept "too much" as a compliment and walk away.

You're exactly who you should be, how you should be, and where you should be. Welcome to the uproarious world of being too fucking much.

If you're like so many other glitterbombs who are slowly, carefully reclaiming their sparkle, it may take some time to really feel like your whole self again.

I recently checked in with a former client about how we've both found big and small ways to bring our truest, most colorful selves into the work and life situations we encounter. We chatted about our IIVs. We lamented the exhaustion that accompanies being something beyond the traditional and expected. We talked about the limbs we walk out on and then cling to as we will new ways of thinking and behaving and approaching stuff into existence.

And then she made a statement about herself and her current colleagues that floored me:

They don't deserve all of me.

I literally heard a record scratch. My mouth went dry. All of the cliches, they happened.

They don't deserve all of me.

She's right. The time and energy we expend being flexible and nimble and welcoming compromise-for-the-sake-of-little-gains…

They don't deserve it, glitterbombs.

Too often, the All Of You that you've fought so hard to confidently bring along throughout every element of your life is a gift that others don't deserve.

The work, the effort, the strength, and the bravery it takes to audaciously, proudly step out as you, may be too much for them because they haven't earned you.

They haven't provided a safe place for you to spread out as yourself.

They haven't cleared space for you to take to the stage and speak loudly and boldly.

They haven't done their own work to prepare for your boss bitch energy.

None of this is about you. Really.

If you're bringing all of you — the glorious, luminescent, brilliant soul — and they're not worthy, don't panic.

Don't stop, either. Showing up as your full, unfiltered self is a radical act of self-respect—and not everyone is entitled to it.

Being your whole self doesn't mean laying every part of who you are on the table for spaces that haven't earned it. It's not hiding, it's strategy. Calibrate. Choose where to invest your energy, where to bring the full spotlight of your presence, and where to let your brilliance shimmer just enough without wasting our light on those who refuse to see it.

So what does calibration actually look like? It might mean dressing in your full vivacious glory for a creative offsite with your internal team, but opting for a sleeker version of your look when presenting to a conservative board—still you, just strategically styled. It could be sharing bold, personal stories in a coaching session, but holding those same stories back in a newer social setting where they don't deserve all of you because the trust hasn't been earned yet. One of my clients is a powerhouse leader who swears like a sailor. With her direct reports and internal Slack? She's delightfully profane. But when she's presenting to the city council, she swaps out her fucks for sharp, playful sarcasm—same spirit, slanted strategy. It's not masking. It's precision. Different setting, different dial.

Let me be very clear: This isn't about shrinking. It's about discernment. It's knowing the difference between playing small and protecting your prismatic energy for the spaces and people who have *earned* it. Boundaries are not barriers; they are a form of self-preservation. Science backs it up. Studies on emotional labor and authentic leadership highlight that constantly performing to meet external expectations, especially in spaces that don't support diversity of thought or identity, erodes your energy, your confidence, and your connection to yourself (Grandey, 2000; Gardner, Cogliser, Davis, & Dickens, 2011). Burnout is inevitable when you're pouring your full brilliance into places that were never designed to hold it.

Which we don't do here.

Allow yourself the moment to pause and then give yourself the gift of enough. Enough of you that you're still honoring who you are, without pushing yourself through the cheese grater of their nonsense. Enough that you're not denying who you are or what you're up to without giving them the room to ignite the burnout fuse.

Don't stop being who you are. But don't push beyond what's safe, what's healthy, and what's worthwhile if they don't deserve all of you.

The ones who do, they're out there.

⁂

Here's where you sparkle

This one's gonna feel tough, so do your best. You don't have to show anyone this work.

I know you will

STEP 1

Because we just need to get this out of the way, set a timer for three minutes. During that minute, tear out the next page and write down everything external that gets in the way of being everything you are. When you're done, light it on fire. Shred it. Throw it away. You've said its name and acknowledged the obstacle. Now, let it go.

Tear out this page!

STEP 2:

Set a timer again for three minutes. Write down everything that happens when you're in the zone and you're operating as your most extra self. Let it flow.

_____

_____

_____

_____

_____

_____

STEP 3

Set the timer for a final three minutes. Then, brag about yourself. The brag must be true. Don't demur. Don't compare. This brag list is not a list of things that you like about yourself — it is a list of your talents, skills, and accomplishments.

_____

_____

_____

_____

_____

_____

WANNA SPARKLE MORE? Set this list aside for a day when you're not feeling it. Invite others to write their own lists AND share your lists out loud to each other.

STEP 4

Now it's time to reflect. How much of your zone of genius contributes to your brag list? How does reviewing your brags hype you up to get more done, to lean in differently, and to proudly own your Extra power? Where is there a gap or some difference between your zone and your brags?

_____

_____

_____

_____

_____

WANNA SPARKLE MORE? Are there tracks from your But-What-If mixtape that can be "taped over" based on your hype list? Have you discovered new evidence that the stories you tell about yourself no longer apply to how you're actually going about getting shit done?

_____

_____

_____

_____

7

Productivity Without Punishment

Coming out of the COVID-19 lockdown, the name of the game has been Productivity, and glitterbomb: I'm already exhausted. It's not yet burnout, because when I set aside time to rest, I feel recharged. But FFS: what are we racing towards?

We both know this P is capitalized.

Just for giggles, I Googled "Productivity & Business Owners" and almost passed out when I saw there were 94,500,000 results and the majority are about how to become more productive. For comparison, when I adjusted my search results to Personal Productivity, it yielded over 243 million-with-an-m responses, and again the majority were about how to become *more* productive.

This is hustle culture. This is, no relief from your IIV getting really loud to let you know that your "good enough" isn't good enough. This is never escaping from perfectionism, and contributing to capitalist, white supremacist systems of oppression.

At some point, there's an invisible line that high achievers, high performers, and high producers cross. After you cross that line, there's this sense that you should have it all figured out, that you should just know what to do, that you're prepared and equipped to answer all the questions to handle all the crises and challenges, to know what's next. And to have it like that <snaps fingers>, at your disposal.

It's the Cult of Should. "I *should* know how to do this thing." Well, who fucking says so? That is an unfair, external, preconditioned oppression that we put on ourselves.

The "Cult of Should" removes your ability to play, to experiment, to fail and to learn. It makes you fall into the hype of hustle culture.

However, It's really important for high achievers, for high performers, for high producers to feel safe, warm, unjudged, and welcomed when you look for support. It's okay that you haven't yet discovered a safe way to be yourself. It's okay that you don't know how to translate who you are on the inside to your business or how you go about your bizness on the outside. It's absolutely okay that you've tried so many Things hoping to feel like they fit you.

It's okay to realize you want something else for yourself and not know what it is or how to get it because you've been a member of the "Cult of Shoulds." But it's not ok to stay there.

Because we are so conditioned to think that productivity is good, we overlook the negative consequences associated with too much productivity, like:

- *Health issues:* Constantly working without taking breaks can result in physical health problems such as fatigue, headaches, and back pain. It can also lead to mental health issues such as anxiety and depression.

- *Reduced creativity:* When individuals are too focused on productivity, they may neglect to take breaks and engage in activities that promote creativity. This can lead to a reduction in innovative ideas and solutions.

- *Strained relationships:* Prioritizing work over personal relationships can cause conflict with family, friends, and romantic partners.

- *Decreased quality:* Focusing solely on productivity may lead to a decrease in the quality of work produced. Rushing to complete tasks quickly can result in mistakes, oversights, and errors.

I'm looking at you, podcasts and books and DIY courses that insist if we could only optimize/multitask/wake up earlier/hustle constantly and faster. It's bullshit. We've conditioned by capitalist systems to think our worth is tied to output, and productivity media plays into that by promising hacks, tricks, and miracle routines that will "fix" our inefficiencies. But the real problem? The system itself. Not you.

Overworking yourself to achieve high productivity can lead to burnout, and burnout can result in feelings of detachment, cynicism, and reduced productivity. In long, productivity can be toxic. Let me give you two very real client examples:

George reached out for coaching because he wanted a healthier work-life at home, especially since he was mostly remote. His evenings had turned into a familiar trap: he'd sit down to "just send one more email," but then another email notification would ping, a spreadsheet would call his name, and before he knew it, two hours had vanished. His dinner would be cold, his (unhappy) wife would be in bed already, and George would be left eating reheated leftovers straight from the microwave, scrolling through Slack like a zombie. It wasn't about ambition: it was about the quiet, gnawing guilt that he wasn't "caught up." It wasn't about ambition: it was about guilt. Somewhere along the way, he'd internalized the idea that being "done" meant being perfect: inbox at zero, to-do list crushed, loose ends neatly tied with a bow. But here's the thing: that level of done? It doesn't exist. And chasing it was costing him the healthy life and relationships he was working so hard to support.

Maria came to coaching because she was at a breaking point with boundary-setting and leaving work at work. Her mornings were a warning sign she didn't want to read: waking up with pounding headaches, shoulders locked up like she'd spent the night in a boxing ring, and a body that screamed for mercy. But instead of slowing down, Maria would chug another iced coffee, swipe on some concealer to fake looking alive, and pep-talk to her reflection *"I don't have time for this."* She pushed through, day after day, treating exhaustion like just another checkbox on her to-do list. At first, no one else noticed. She was still meeting deadlines, still delivering, still showing up. But the spark that made her great—the creativity, the thoughtfulness, the extra layer of magic? It started to flicker out. By the time she finally closed her laptop at night, Maria wasn't celebrating wins anymore. She was just surviving. And the most heartbreaking part? Even then, she wondered if she was doing enough.

George and Maria both fell into the too-much-productivity trap, but in different ways. George's "one last task" habit kept him tethered to his laptop long past quitting time, stealing his evenings and straining his marriage. Maria, on the other hand, ignored her body's warning signs, running on caffeine and sheer willpower until exhaustion tanked both her energy and

Maybe if you're being totally honest, things are slowly creeping up on you, too?

her work quality. They were both chasing an impossible standard that slowly crept into their days until their well-being, relationships, and effectiveness eroded without them noticing until it was too late.

How do you preserve your energy and your resources, and learn to become more intentional and kinder to ourselves and those around you? How do you make intentional space for thought and rest and creativity, ESPECIALLY when the structures around us reward this hustle & hype? Start by remembering this: just because you *can* do it all, doesn't mean you *have to*. Productivity without purpose is just burnout in a cute outfit.

It is because of this reenergized pressure of productivity that too many of my recent client conversations have centered around:

How can I be more productive?

What are some tips you've seen that help boost productivity?

What are some hacks that work?

Now, I know and you know that when you ask me for my opinion, you're really looking for validation, affirmation, and support. And you know that I'm not going to tell you what to do. After all, that's not good coaching. Instead, we begin with these questions:

When I say the word productivity, what do you HEAR?

- A to-do list, a bullet journal page, a stack of post-it notes?
- Your IIV pushing play on the But-What-If mixtape to criticize and stymie you for not doing enough?
- Your body trying to hype up your nervous system to operate in a way that betrays how you best operate?
- Or maybe even, accomplishment, because you're working on things that align with your values? (Go you!)

When you think about productivity, how do you FEEL?

- Tightness in your chest and a mild headache?
- The competitive rush of you-against-the-clock?
- Like you wanna do anything other than what's in your inbox?

Like so many things, the way that you think about productivity and the way that you experience productivity is unique to you. Hacks and tips won't work unless you understand where you're impacted, where you're bogged down, where you're motivated; basically, where you are ready to commit to making a change for yourself.

Then, you have to get really comfortable with what's good enough. You can't be everywhere, and you can't do everything. Discover what's enough — what's sustainably, honestly enough — and set that boundary and hold to it.

And on the off chance you really ARE looking for my opinion, here's what I have for you.

Procrastinate. If you're not ready to start, do something else. Occasionally, the pressure of "I have no more time left so I have to do this" is the fire you need to get something done.

Organize your space. You don't have to have a tidy workspace to get things done. But you do need to have a workspace that's conducive to working. Got your favorite mug? Your notebook and pen? Your laptop charger? A safe space to work? What will you actually need to have around you in order to work efficiently? Reward future you with prepping your space.

My partner can always pinpoint when I'm fretting about a task when I do ALL THE LAUNDRY from start to finish (which includes putting it away).

Eliminate distractions. Seriously, turn off the notifications, the dings and bings, close the blinds, send the dog to their crate, put on noise-canceling headphones, return that phone call... whatever you need to do in order to be able to focus on what's ahead of you instead of getting sidetracked by the world outside.

I use a paper planner, because sometimes the old ways are the best ways. But I also have a digital calendar because I'm not a complete monster.

Start with your can-dos. My planner is frequently out of control. I have to get very real with myself about what I have the capacity and capability to do, and when. My ambition may be exponential, but my time and my energy are limited, savvy? In those moments when you're ready to stare down your to-do list, ask yourself what must be done today and what's driving that timeline? What has the most value or priority to you? What's on your list that you didn't want to agree to in the first place, and how can you offload it? Pick one part of one thing and start there.

Give yourself a time limit. 12 minutes. 1 half hour. 2 hours. 7 email responses. 4 calls. Whatever feels right and fits how you best work. I know so many people who swear by the pomodoro technique; I'm not one of them. Who cares?! Give yourself an endpoint; it's then your choice whether you stop working or keep going.

Build a soundtrack. This one's deeply personal. I used to play music constantly when I was working, mostly so I could ignore it (a strange method of focusing, but it worked for me). Now I'm in a season of doing that less. But if you like to have something going in the background, there are a couple of different approaches. You can always go the classical music route (brain food, I've been told). You can put on your favorite jams that pump you up and keep you moving. You can listen to EDM or house or your favorite DJ's set on YouTube or the sound of whales migrating or nothing at all.

Fuel your body. I'm big on snacks. Have something at the ready to nourish your tummy and your mind. And don't forget to hydrate.

Change your scenery, intentionally. Maybe stick your head outside for some fresh air. Move around the room or around your block. Take a disco nap. Wiggle. Don't get stuck in one place. You've already imprinted there enough.

Real talk: We tend to focus on maximizing our time and energy in order to get shit done. We may deprioritize tasks based on our interests, needs, and preferences, in favor of doing something for others. There's a lot of pressure to do it all and have it all. Who hasn't heard:

"Just manage your time better!"

"Time block your calendar."

"Talk to your manager about what can come off your plate."

"Delegate tasks at home, too!"

Glitterbomb, just typing all that is making my nervous system... nervous.

Look, I want you to unlock your full potential and become a productivity powerhouse, but I don't want you to do it at the risk of your own well-being. And I know you don't want that, either.

I invite you to come to healthier terms with productivity by focusing on what you're excited about, what lights you up, what inspires a happy dance. You'll be motivated, energized, and excited to get things done, and that will carry over to other tasks. HELL YES is the greatest productivity hack of all.

Here's where you sparkle

Glitterbomb, I don't want to leave you with philosophy and "thought leadership" and positivity when you have to deliver for others, so let's get practical.

Here's where we start: with what's real and meaningful to us. If we start with ourselves, then we'll have a better barometer moving forward of where we should focus our time, energy and resources — where we can proclaim productivity — and where we should deflect, decline, or delegate.

STEP 1:

Set a timer for 3 minutes, and answer these questions:

What do you value and what matters to you?

_____

_____

_____

_____

What impact do you want to have?

_____

_____

_____

_____

How are you getting in your own way?

_____

_____

_____

_____

Now that we've refreshed ourselves, our impacts, and our own nonsense, let's take it to task-setting.

STEP 2

Take a look at next week:

What's ONE thing you absolutely must get done? — this is often for someone else (i.e., a client, your kid, the community, etc.)

_____

What's one thing you WANT to do? — this is often some form of business administration or household management

_____

What's one thing you WOULD LIKE to do? — this is personal

_____

Now ideally, this is three tasks per week, but I've found that the overachievers and high producers panic and pivot this to three tasks per day. I challenge you to keep this simple and streamlined. You can always add more later; it's harder to take away. Set a timer for 3 minutes and answer these questions to identify The Big 3.

STEP 3

Looking at your Big 3, where do you imagine you may experience a roadblock? How can you preempt this before it actually interferes with your progress? What commitment are you prepared to make to yourself to stick with your 3 and disrupt your own toxic productivity habits?

_____

_____

_____

_____

_____

_____

Because if it's never enough, then you're never enough.

8

Perfect In Your Imperfections

I'm a recovering perfectionist.

I know. You're SHOCKED.

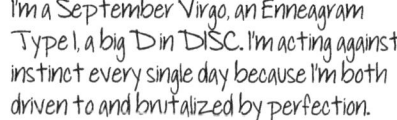

I'm a September Virgo, an Enneagram Type 1, a big D in DISC. I'm acting against instinct every single day because I'm both driven to and brutalized by perfection.

And for many, many years, I tried to convince myself and a lot of people around me that I was a healthy perfectionist. I wouldn't start doing things or learning new things unless I knew that I could do them. Really, really well.

I also would work and overwork and rework tasks and work deliverables that were potentially good enough already because I had unrealistic expectations, or I wanted to go above and beyond. I didn't want to under-promise and under-deliver so I always over-promised and over-delivered. Sound familiar, Reader?

In the long run, I was exhausting myself trying to achieve something for myself that was potentially unattainable.

According to Psychology Today, high-achieving women are especially prone to this relentless pressure, driving themselves to exhaustion in the name of getting it right (Wright, 2025). The kicker? That constant striving isn't just stressful — it can lead to migraines, chronic fatigue, and a whole host of stress-related health issues. The biggest lie we tell ourselves is that perfectionism is a gold star in life. It isn't. It's a high-stakes hustle that keeps us playing small and holds us back wellness-wise in the long run.

The real win? Cutting yourself some slack so that you can actually live, breathe, and thrive instead of just performing "success." Set some realistic 'I Wants' that don't add more stress to your life. Find ways to shush your IIV so that you are not competing against an unrealistic image of yourself in your own mind.

As you're doing your work day-to-day, your perfectionism is holding you back. It's keeping you from doing things that you might find fun, or that might help you grow in ways you cannot imagine.

Figure out what really is the best that you can do. Because — I shit you not — the best that you can do is really the absolute best.

It's more than enough.

It's more than good enough.

Find and celebrate the imperfections because that's what will make it memorable; the little blips, the little hiccups, the things that you learn from "fail hard, fail harder."

You're taught that failure is something to be afraid of, to stay away from. If you want to innovate, if you want to drive your industry, and if you want to supercharge your life, you have to get over failure-as-bad real quick. Instead, consider failure as a series of iterations to get something closer to "right." Within those iterations, explore with humility, and an open heart and mind.

With failure comes risks, and with risks come opportunities. Failing is getting out of your own way to be able to see what's next. Failing builds character and focuses the journey. Don't be shy: fail really fucking hard.

The moment you shed this idea of "I have to do it right," you will grow and explore and have joy in the day-to-day things. It isn't just about reducing stress; it's about fostering creativity and resilience. When we let go of the need to be flawless, we open ourselves up to experimenting with new approaches and ideas without the fear of judgment. Each misstep or error becomes a valuable learning opportunity rather than a mark of failure. By accepting that mistakes are a natural part of any process, we create an environment where innovation can flourish. Instead of seeing imperfections as shortcomings, we start to view them as essential components of growth and personal development.

Keep pushing boundaries, celebrate your progress, and most importantly, give yourself permission to be imperfect. Your journey towards embracing imperfection will not only make your path more enjoyable but will also inspire others to do the same.

From one recovering perfectionist to another, it is very, very possible to practice letting go of your perfectionist tendencies and just enjoy being the incredible badass that you actually are. May you be perfect in your imperfections.

***
Here's where you sparkle

One of the keys to conquering perfectionism is understanding what's important to focus on, and what to let go of. That's where my Very Favorite Activity comes in.

It's called the Sphere of Influence. Sometimes, when you do the hard work to establish tight boundaries, clarify priorities, and embrace imperfection, you slam into external factors that interfere with how you want to go about your business. This exercise helps to drive your success and to ensure that you are ignoring the things that will get in your way and focus on the things that are truly within your sphere.

1. *The Sphere:* Set a timer for 3 minutes. In the circle on the next page, write the elements that you can directly touch, you can push, you can pull, you can adjust. These are the things that in the day-to-day are tangible to you, like your behavior, your actions, your words, your relationships, etc. These are the things that you can govern yourself. Don't edit yourself. Don't try to solve problems. Just brainstorm.

2. *The Box:* Reset the timer for another 3 minutes. Outside of your sphere is a box. This box represents elements that are completely out of your control. The weather, for example, is out of your control. In the box but outside of the circle, write the things that are completely out of your control. Again, don't edit yourself. Just write.

3. *The Reflection:* Take a moment to really reflect on what is within your control; what is within the sphere. This is where you can have the most impact. This is where you can make progress and take ownership of your goals or have influence on what's outside. This is where you can start to put things into practice and then watch the beautiful ripple or cascade or sparkle effect out to the things that are out of your control. That's where the work happens: within the sphere.

Did anything jump out to you as you were completing your sphere? Any surprises?

In considering what's OUTSIDE of your sphere, is there anything you want to add to the sphere itself to help influence your external factors?

_____

_____

_____

_____

_____

_____

_____

9

Burned To A Crisp

Let me tell you a quick story. During the first week of September in 2021, I felt like I just couldn't win. My allergies were acting up and I was sleeping worse than normal. I was working longer hours than I should have, (im)balancing some 20-25 hours of consulting work with 6-10 hours of coaching and 4-8 hours of virtual teaching. It was also the era of COVID quarantine, which meant that everything just felt harder.

And along the way I allowed my boundaries to be compromised, and I didn't tend to things that would have supported my health and well-being.

I was Not Myself.

That Friday afternoon I received some news that in ordinary circumstances would have bummed me out for 20 minutes, and then I would have wiggled it out, regrouped, and bounced back. But on that day, there was no bouncing. I broke, hard. I started crying and couldn't stop. I felt such disappointment and had no healthy place to channel it to — and I felt like there wasn't an option to take time to cope/heal/recover. Worst of all, I couldn't separate myself as a person from the business impact that I was experiencing.

Instead, I did what any logical Virgo would do in a moment of overwhelm: I started moving furniture. I moved my desk 90 degrees. Without unloading a bookshelf that is easily two feet taller than me, I started lugging it around to the opposite wall. I dragged and pushed a small sofa out of the way, which meant that it then was wedged half in/half out of the room. I ordered paint online from our local big box home improvement store, and I ordered wallpaper. I pulled out pictures and art and certificates that had been in a tidy little pile waiting while I found them a home and started putting nails in the wall to make a gallery of them.

All while still crying.

Finally, maybe an hour after all of this started, my partner discovered me sitting at my newly moved desk sobbing while putting spin art from the nieces and nephews into picture frames. No defenses. No resiliency. Just a big ol' overtired, overbaked, overworked puddle. He made me stop, get some fresh air and some water and a snack, and talk about it.

Glitterbomb: raise your hand if you've ever burned the candle at both ends?

Cool.

Now raise your other hand if you've ever cut the candle in half to have more ends to burn?

Ah, my people.

Finally, raise your hand if you burned so bright you lost sleep and control over your emotions and didn't eat well and became the very worst version of yourself?

Hello, you burned-out soul.

Burnout happens when ambitious people accept that "unhealthy busy" is the drumbeat of their lives. So, we're all defining it the same way, this is what I mean when I talk about burnout: "Burnout is a state of emotional, mental, and often physical exhaustion brought on by prolonged or repeated stress."

Herbert Freudenberger is credited with saying this.

I'm not talking about people who like to have full schedules. I'm talking about and to the people who double- or triple-book themselves; shelve their personal priorities and goals to make room for things that don't really matter to them; and commit to projects or relationships or endeavors that hold hostage their energy, spirit and joy.

You know when you're saying things like, "If I don't do XYZ, I'm gonna burn out?" Glitterbomb, if you're saying that out loud, you've already crossed that threshold. You're there. You're burnt.

Were there red flags along the way? Sure enough, but you were so singularly focused on trying to survive that your heart couldn't catch up to your brain and your hands. If you take a moment to think about the last time you felt totally burned out, can you find the flags along the way?

For me, it starts with slight queasiness in my stomach. It's that feeling of impending doom; a "run away" sense that my brain and my heart know I'm about to blatantly ignore because I don't want to disappoint, make someone mad, or worry that my integrity will be questioned. I'm about to actively kick my carefully crafted boundaries to the curb. I'm saying yes to something that I don't want to say yes to.

Where does it start with you?

Overachievers, high performers, golden children: we do this a lot. We receive a request and every fiber of our being screams "NO," but we meekly agree to whatever the request is that's been presented to us. And then we lose sleep, lose income and lose precious me-time satisfying the needs of others. We abandon carefully crafted boundaries for a variety of reasons, and we take far too many steps closer to burnout.

Ugh, even typing this makes me want to puke.

Go with me on this journey:

Close your eyes (or, you know... don't if you don't want to)

Take a breath. Take another.

Think about the last three days.

What are the moments when you reluctantly agreed to something that you weren't really interested in doing, that hijacked your time, or that created unhealthy conflict within you? What signals were your mind, your body and your heart giving you that "yes" wasn't It? Did you listen?

What has that choice brought to you?

For me, I've said "yes" when I wanted to say "no" three times in the last three days. That's way more queasiness than a girl needs.

The "yes" has brought in work that I'm not passionate about and has taken time away from my family. I deserve to treat myself, my business and those who are important to me better than that.

You can read articles across Huffington Post and Harvard Business Review, and watch a bunch of TED Talks that all offer the same solutions: Set and honor your boundaries. Seek support. Prioritize yourself.

Nothing new there, right?

Not exactly. Here's the tough thing: to honor your boundaries, you have to say no. To get support, you have to create limits for people who take more than they give. To prioritize yourself, you have to make critical choices about how and where to spend your time.

You have to get to know your No.

What motivates you? What's important to you? What are you reaching for and moving towards every day? Now, flip those questions: what demotivates you? What's not important or a priority for you and your business? What will get in the way of your progress?

Be really honest with yourself here so that you can protect your squishy nougat center. This could be something as simple as "I'm not agreeing to vacuum the living space on Tuesdays" to something bigger like "We have no availability for new work until June and cannot do a 'favor' for past clients." Hold that line with confidence and when the internal negging starts, think about how you'd talk a friend or colleague through this scenario and then talk to yourself that way, too.

Here's what they don't tell you, so I'm gonna: when you say no to

A quick note here: when you send a declination you don't owe anyone an explanation. I hear this from my clients a lot: "I don't want to do this, but what should I say because I don't want to disappoint them or hurt their feelings." Give yourself a couple of boilerplate responses to have on-hand, 2-3 sentences that sound like you, are polite but firm, and close the door on the request. No explaining necessary.

some Thing, you're actually saying yes to some Thing else. It could be a vacation or a more relaxed opportunity to do your job; it could be room to internally strategize or nourish your personal and professional self. Your time is finite and so is your energy. Spend it on what adds the most value to you.

No matter what, it's not too late to help yourself, and my guess is you're in the best of company. You CAN recover from burnout, and you can start building new practices to prevent burnout from happening.

It's going to take some time to let go of the unhealthy busy and allow the "saying yes to saying no" to settle itself to something manageable and balanced. It's going to take you some time to reclaim your energy and well-being. Just like with acknowledging and ignoring your IIV, you'll find yourself pushing against old habits while you practice new ones.

As for me? I didn't just slap a self-care Band-Aid on my burnout and call it a day. I rebuilt the damn operating system.

Here's what I changed:

I stopped worshiping at the altar of overwork. Hustle culture wanted me to believe that more hours equalled more impact, but burnout showed me the cost of that lie. So, I set boundaries that actually mean something, protecting my time, energy, and brilliance like the rare commodities they are.

I redefined productivity on my terms. Instead of measuring success by how exhausted I was at the end of the day, I started focusing on meaningful progress. More isn't better. Better is better.

I built more breathing room into my life. Burnout was my body throwing a tantrum after years of being ignored. Post-burnout, I gave myself permission to rest, to pause, to enjoy things just because — no ROI required.

I got choosier about who and what gets my energy. No more saying yes out of guilt or obligation. Just because I'm available doesn't mean I'm free. If it doesn't align, excite, or expand me? It's a no. Period.

I leaned into joy, play, and the unexpected. My best ideas, biggest breakthroughs, and happiest moments come when I let go a little. Play

My absolute favorite recipe for bourbon chocolate pecan pie is included at the back of this book. Because it's my book, that's why.

became a non-negotiable, whether that's wrestling with the puppy, travel, or just dancing in my kitchen like no one is watching.

At my core, I'm still the ambitious, driven powerhouse I always was. I just lead with intention now, instead of burnout-fueled autopilot. Because I've already been to the edge, and I'm not interested in going back.

Really, it's like baking a pie, which is a hobby I really enjoy that helps me distract and recover from burnout. It adds joy and movement to times when I'd get grump and stagnant. My first few pies were wonky, and the crust burned at the edges as I was building up new skills and commitments to yourself. But I found my groove and now have good bakes that are Hollywood Handshake-worthy.

Watch out for burns and bake well.

Do you have a hobby that's a version of this? Something that brings joy, distraction, and recovery in crispy times?

✳✳✳

Here's where you sparkle

If you're thinking you're burned out, follow these five steps. Right now. I'll wait.

STEP 1

Put one thing down immediately. Decide on the one thing that matters least in the grand scheme of things and let it go and reclaim that brain-space.

STEP 2

Take a break and take some air. Fresh air. Outside air, if you can. A change of scenery can change your perspective, and a little sun will do you wonders.

STEP 3

Get real with yourself about what's enough. What are you working so hard for? What do you really need? What do you really need to do? Does it have to be done now? (Check back to Chapter 8 if you need a refresher)

STEP 4

Set boundaries and stick to them. For every NO there's a YES. Understand your YES and start moving in that direction.

STEP 5

Be a little nicer to yourself, please and thank you. Get some sleep. Exercise, if it's your thing. Have a snack. Hydrate. Do something that's only for you that makes you happy; turn up the joy.

Remember: we're aiming for practice, not perfection. I AM REALLY SERIOUS ABOUT THIS.

10

Count Your Blessings

I'm rewriting this chapter during a flight home from a working trip to Mexico City. After being 'internet business friends' with two brilliant souls for over four years, we found a week and an Airbnb and a reason to gather: we're all writing books. For a week, these two (plus a partner) and I ate street tacos and co-worked and wrote and laughed and rode bikes and supported each other in-person the way we do through text and Slack. It was gorgeous.

I met Devin and Lex through online networking groups early in my entrepreneurship journey. Not only have I relied on their wisdom and expertise to journey through key phases of my business's growth, but I've relied on their friendship to keep me going through key phases of my business owner growth. We have cross- mentored, collaborated and advocated for each other with generosity and trust. Truly, I wouldn't have made it as far as I have in my business without them. Truly. They're magical, like unicorns.

Let's talk about unicorns. And no, not the sparkly, horned variety. I mean your unicorn herd: the brilliant, dynamic, inspiring people who help you ride the wild wave of life. Glitterbombs — yes, even the introverted ones — don't shine in isolation. We thrive in connection. Your herd is made up of people as sharp, bold, and creative as you are, and together, you multiply each other's impact in ways that make the impossible look like a casual Tuesday. *Though, let's be clear, they're iconic.*

Here's the thing about a unicorn herd: when their powers combine, big dreams become "hold my glitter" moments. A real, thoughtful community is the difference between feeling stuck and starting a movement. That's why I refuse to use the word "network": it's been drained of meaning, or worse, turned into something transactional. We're not here for superficial LinkedIn reactions. We're here for deep, intentional, ride-or-die relationships.

Because here's the truth: you make each other better just by existing in the same orbit. Need someone who spits wisdom like a rainbow when you're stuck? There's a unicorn for that — mine is Devin. Looking for an intro to a dream collaborator? Your unicorns have connections — that's Lex. Having a full-body existential meltdown and need emergency tacos and pep talks? Your comfort unicorn is already en route — hi Rob!

A strong herd isn't just a collection of people. It's a carefully curated ecosystem of different perspectives, skill sets, and lived experiences. That diversity expands your thinking, challenges your blind spots, and keeps you from settling for *meh*. And when things get tough (because let's be real, they always do), they're the ones who remind you who the hell you are. They show up for the hard moments, not just the wins. They help you recalibrate when you're too deep in your own head. Whether it's handing you tissues or lovingly calling you on your bullshit, they get you back to yourself.

Over the years, I've coached groups of powerhouse women at all levels — leaders, creatives, entrepreneurs. And let me tell you, when they first show up, they often think they're failures. They don't have all the answers. They second-guess their instincts. They on-paper have everything but feel guilty for wanting more. They worry they've wasted too much time on the wrong thing. But once they get past the "get to know you" stage — once they let themselves be real and vulnerable — they realize that every single person in the room is dealing with some version of the same damn thing. There's a collective sigh of relief. They're not alone anymore. And that's when the real fun begins.

Having a unicorn herd makes you memorable. The best leaders don't just make waves — they create a ripple effect that outlives them. Their legacy isn't in solo achievements; it's in the people they lifted up, the doors they opened, the relationships they nurtured. The people in your herd will talk about your impact long after you've moved on to your next adventure. They'll say, "That person changed my life." And not because you were the smartest or the loudest in the room — but because you *showed up* for people, built something bigger than yourself, and made space for others to rise.

So how do you build your unicorn herd?

Be generous with your time. Spend time with people who inspire you. Learn from them. Offer your help without expecting anything in return. "How can I show up for you?" is one of my favorite questions.

Create space for vulnerability. Don't be a superhero. Admit when you need help and lean on your herd for support.

Invest in relationships. Just like any great partnership, community requires care. Send a check-in text, show appreciation, and be there when it counts.

You won't stand out just because you have bold ideas or an impressive résumé. You'll stand out because you've cultivated a legendary community. One that you can rely on, learn from, and grow with. So, gather your herd. Nurture those connections. And let the magic of collaboration take you to the next level.

After all, a blessing of unicorns is way more powerful than a lone wolf. And infinitely more vibrant.

Yes, that's their collective noun.

So, to count those blessings:

- The higher you rise, the lonelier it can be. Find your sounding board for differing points of view and perspective.

- Expand your community beyond the usual people you see every day or every year at that industry conference. Be curious about other people's stories and how they can inform your own. Give more than you receive.

- Community brings relief regardless of level. Whether somebody's a CEO or starting their first artistic pursuit, I've seen beautiful, wild relief in their face when they realize their doubts and hangups are in their heads — not an innate inability to succeed. You're not alone, even when it feels lonely.

- The moment you're willing to vulnerably reach up and out for help is the moment your growth becomes exponential. That's when we get out of our own way so people can lovingly call us on our bullshit, empathize with us, and get us turned around so we can dominate another day.

✳✳✳
Here's where you sparkle

Advocates, collaborators, and mentors. They hold the key to your success, and they're critical to your growth into the legendary glitterbomb I know you are. They're an essential part of your herd.

So, we're gonna keep this one simple. Define each of these terms for yourself:

Advocate _____

Collaborator _____

Mentor _____

Next, flip through your internal Rolodex and list 3-5 names for each category.

Advocate

1. _____

2. _____

3. _____

4. _____

5. _____

Collaborator

1. _____

2. _____

3. _____

4. _____

5. _____

Mentor

1. _____

2. _____

3. _____

4. _____

5. _____

Then think about where your 'I Want' is taking you. Do these folks know what you're working on? How would they show up for you if you told them? Do you need to add or replace names to get you where you want to be?

_____

_____

_____

_____

_____

_____

WANNA SPARKLE MORE? Who would consider you an Advocate, Collaborator, or Mentor? When was the last time you connected with them, just to say hi?

WANNA SPARKLE MOST? Think of the Advocates, Collaborators, and Mentors in your life, who have supported you through the tensions and triumphs. Have you told them how much their support has meant, or what impact they've had on you? Because now's as good a time as any to throw a little glitter at them.

11

Let's Wrap This Up

Dearest Glitterbomb,

You did it. You made it to the end of this book.

But really? You've arrived at the beginning of something even bigger. A bold, radiant, *unapologetic* you. One that owns your brilliance, trusts your instincts, and refuses to shrink to fit. This journey wasn't about becoming someone new. It was about becoming *more* of who you've always been.

And along the way, you built a toolkit. Every exercise, every reflection, every step you took built upon the one before it, layering clarity, confidence, and courage into your foundation. The Given Circumstances helped you examine where you came from, your 'I Want' statement clarified where you're going, and The Funknown™ made space for you to embrace the messy, magnificent in-between as you're growing towards 'I Am'. You unwound the But-What-If Mixtape, redefined productivity on your own terms, and gave yourself permission to choose *you*, without waiting for external validation.

But this isn't just about you. It never was.

Something shifts when you finally, really see yourself as capable, worthy, and already enough. The second you step into that power; you begin to notice glimmers of it in others. You'll see it in a colleague hesitating to speak up in a meeting, in a friend playing small, in a stranger's nervous excitement about something new. And here's where the magic happens: because you've walked this path, *you get to be the one who hands them a little extra sparkle.*

Legacies aren't built wins and workarounds alone. They're built in the micro-moments: those conversations where you remind someone of their brilliance, the invitations you extend to help others rise, the space you create for people to bring their full selves to the table. Just by being your truest, most colorful self, you are giving others permission to do the same. That's how movements start. That's how we rewrite the rules. That's how we change the world, one glitterbomb at a time.

By now, your perspective on goals has probably shifted, too. Goals aren't checkboxes. They aren't rigid timelines. They aren't proof of worthiness. Goals are guiding stars, illuminating the path forward while leaving space for surprise, evolution, and expansion. You know that real success isn't about perfection. It's about movement. Growth. Experimentation. *Play*. You don't have to have it all figured out before you begin. You just have to begin.

You also know that you're not doing this alone. Your unicorn herd is out there — your advocates, mentors, and collaborators — ready to celebrate your wins, challenge your limits, and pick you up when you stumble. And guess what? You *get* to be that person for someone else, too.

Find your people. Take up space. Show up boldly. And above all, keep making loud, unapologetic noise in a world that needs your sparkle.

Now go forth and be legendary. The world is so much brighter with you in it.

Kari

Here's where you sparkle, one last time

Take a moment right now to reflect on what resonated with you most. What's one thing you're taking with you from these pages? Write it down. Say it out loud. Share it with a friend.

_____

_____

_____

_____

_____

_____

_____

_____

_____

_____

_____

_____

And then? Go make some noise.

✳

You're at the beginning, not the end.

I wrote this book with hope under my fingernails and post-it notes on every surface. And while it's packed with tools I use with clients, it's also full of tools I still use myself. I'm still saying NO to things that don't fit. I'm still challenging my IIV. I'm still exploring The Funknown™ and figuring out what productivity without punishment looks like — especially on the days when I'd rather nap. The most resonant feedback I've received from readers and clients alike is this: "I feel seen." If that's true for you too, I hope you'll tell me. That's where the glitter sticks.

Bibliography

Aristotle. *Poetics*. Edited by S.H. Butcher, MacMillan and Co., 1902.

Clance, P. R. (n.d.). *The impostor phenomenon in high achieving women: Dynamics and therapeutic intervention*. Retrieved February 19, 2025, from https://www.paulincroseclance.com/pdf/ip_high_achieving_women.pdf

Collier, L. (2016, November). *Growth after trauma*. American Psychological Association.

Wikipedia contributors. (n.d.). *Human condition*. Wikipedia, The Free Encyclopedia. Retrieved February 19, 2025, from https://en.wikipedia.org/wiki/Human_condition

Cooley, Charles Horton. *Human Nature and the Social Order*. Charles Scribner's Sons, 1922.

Davis, Joseph E. (2021, April 27). *Is Authenticity Still an Ideal?* Psychology Today.

Gardner, W.L., Cogliser, C.C., Davis, K.M., & Dickens, M.P. (2011). *Authentic leadership: A review of the literature and research agenda*. Leadership Quarterly, 22, 1120-1145.

Grandey, Alicia A. *Emotion Regulation in the Workplace: A New Way to Conceptualize Emotional Labor*. Journal of Occupational Health Psychology, vol. 5, no. 1, Feb. 2000, pp. 95-110.

New York Film Academy. (n.d.). *Stanislavski in 7 steps: Better understanding Stanislavski's 7 questions*. NYFA Student Resources. Retrieved February 19, 2025, from https://www.nyfa.edu/student-resources/stanislavski-in-7-

steps-better-understanding-stanisklavskis-7-questions/

Shakespeare, William. *The Riverside Shakespeare*. Edited by G. Blakemore Evans et al., Houghton Mifflin, 1974.

Stamarski, C. S., & Son Hing, L. S. (2015). *Gender inequalities in the workplace: The effects of organizational structures, processes, practices, and decision makers' sexism*. Frontiers in Psychology, 6, Article 1400.

Whiting, N. (2024, April 11). *The power of embracing uncertainty*. Psychology Today.

WOI+ Editorial Team. (2024, August 12). *The hidden impact of gender norms on leadership*. Women of Influence.

Women of Influence. (n.d.). *The tallest poppy*. Retrieved February 19, 2025, from https://www.womenofinfluence.ca/tps/

Wright, A. (2025, February 4). *Overcoming perfectionism in high-achieving women*. Psychology Today.

Kari's Favorite Bourbon Chocolate Pecan Pie Recipe

INGREDIENTS FOR THE PIE CRUST

LOOK, Pillsbury brand piecrust is the bomb. Use that if baking your own dough feels a little too much, ok?

- 2 1/2 cups all-purpose flour (if you're GF, Bob's Red Mill has a fantastic all-purpose GF flour that's a 1:1 substitute)
- 1 teaspoon salt
- 1 teaspoon granulated sugar
- 2 sticks chilled butter, cut into pieces (I use one stick salted and one stick unsalted, but you do you)
- 1/4 to 1/2 cup ice water

INGREDIENTS FOR THE PIE FILLING

- 1/2 cup light brown sugar, lightly packed
- 1/2 cup granulated sugar
- 1/2 cup all-purpose flour
- a little pinch Kosher salt (to flavor)
- 1 stick unsalted butter, melted and slightly cooled
- 2 extra-large eggs
- 1 teaspoon pure vanilla extract
- 2 1/2 tablespoons good bourbon (LMK if you need suggestions)
- 1–1/4 cups semisweet chocolate chips
- 1 cup large-diced pecans, plus whole pecans for to make a decorative top

MAKE THE PIE DOUGH

1. Mix the dry ingredients together in a large bowl by hand (or in a stand mixer)

2. Work in the butter a few pieces at a time, until the mixture starts to resemble playground sand

3. Add 4 tablespoons of ice water, and work (with your hands or a dough paddle) until the dough comes together. Don't overwork. You'll still see little clumps of butter here and there

4. Set your oven to 375 degrees F

5. Cut the dough in half and smush into little disks. Wrap them separately in plastic wrap and let them rest in the fridge for an hour.
NOTE: If you have a deep pie dish, you may not want to cut the dough

6. Roll out the dough so that it will fit into the bottom of your pie dish and drape over the sides by about an inch (you may have to trim the dough)

7. Line the bottom of the crust with parchment paper and fill with pie weights or dried beans

8. Blind bake (or par bake_)the crust until it juuuuust starts to brown, usually 7–8 minutes.

9. Let cool and remove the pie weights.

10. This can be done up to 3 days before you make the pie filling — it will keep wrapped up in the fridge.

MAKE THE FILLING, AND PUT IT ALL TOGETHER

11. Pre-heat the oven to 350 degrees F

12. Combine the brown sugar, granulated sugar, flour, and seat in a medium bowl

13. Whisk together the butter, eggs, vanilla, and bourbon in a small bowl

14. Pour the liquid ingredients into the dry ingredients and stir until combined (This is not a Moira Rose "folding" moment. Really let those ingredients get to know each other)

15. Stir in the chocolate chips and pecan pieces

16. Pour the filling into the blind baked pie crust. NOTE: if the filling looks really, really wet, use a slotted spoon to scoop the filling into the shell first, and then add some of the remaining baking liquid. You don't want a soupy pie.

    I like to make a decorative topping with whole pecans, but we all know I'm a lot. So do what feels right

17. Bake for 35-40 minutes until the top looks golden brown and the filling is as firm in the middle as it is on the edge.

Cool. Serve. Enjoy.

*

Acknowledgements

This book wouldn't exist without Connor Hogan and their ability to get me to do things I dream about but hold myself back from. Connor supported the creation of Uproar Coaching's branding, and they doula'd the hell outta this book. They also made me do movement-based activities to shake themes loose. I am forever indebted to their beautiful face, brilliant mind, and wicked humor.

Two Kates ushered this book across the publish line: Kate Mosesso edited this book from glimmer to glitterbomb, challenging me on shape and form and everything in between; 3 squeezes. Kate Christy arrived with a hell yes to design the very experience you're holding — and she did so with excellence, humor, and care to carry Uproar into its pages.

Thank you to the glitterbombs who prop me up every day: Devin Lee, Lex Roman, Jennifer O'Sullivan, Janna Carlson, Bev Feldman, Chantelle Davis-Gray, Ali Daniels, Jess Milanes and Tania Bhattacharyya. If you're a business owner and you don't know them, you're doing yourself a huge disservice.

Thank you, Megan Thrift and Heather Haney and Rana Kay and Bess Kaye and Dani Stoller. To the Fam for dinner and movies, and Definitely Not Cheating for trivia shenanigans.

Thank you Mimsi Janis (and Godiva). Because we don't 'do feelings', I'll just leave it at this. Because she knows and she's in my will.

Thank you, Sophia Casey who mentored me into being a great coach.

Thank you, Cheryl Newberger who showed me how to lead with patience, understanding, excellence and kindness. Who never, ever tried to change me but sought to understand and enhance me. We should all be lucky to have been led by Cheryl.

Thanks to my mom, Erika Ginsburg, for reminding me that I'm clever and kind and talented. She let me be loud and weird, she supported my artistry and celebrated my view of the world. She believed.

Thank you, Britten Pund, my polar-opposite sister. We've had quite the ride and I'm so very thankful for the relationship we have. You inspire me.

Thank you to the Finleys, who accepted me into their family like one of their own. They didn't have to, and I'm so, so very lucky you did.

The biggest thanks to my brilliant Renaissance man: James Finley. You believed I had a book in me and wouldn't let me wave it off. You've kept me fed with grilled cheese, spicy chips, Cherry Coke, and Sour Patch Kids. My life is so much richer for having you in it, and I'm so thankful you didn't blink or balk when I said I wanted to launch my business at the start of a global pandemic. Maybe no one will read this book, but I know you've read every single word and argued with me over every gd comma. Thank you, love of my life. You've made me better.

And finally, to the Glitterbombs. This uproarious community. Every time you connect with me for support, I am reminded of the privilege of showing up with you as you're reaching for something great that's entirely for you. Thank you for your trust, for your spirit of adventure, and your vulnerability.

You're so badass.

*

About the Author

Kari Ginsburg (she/her) is a dog mom and proud aunt, a used-bookstore lover, and backyard beekeeper, and true crime obsessive, and a brain tumor survivor, and an award-winning actor. She's a trauma-informed Professional Certified Executive & Life Coach through the International Coaching Federation; and she's one of the first 500 people in the world to become a Certified Change Management Professional through the Association of Change Management Professionals. In 2024 and 2025 she was recognized as a Top Executive Coach in Washington, DC, and in 2025 that recognition was expanded to a Top Coach in America. She lives in the Washington, DC region with her partner, her pittie rescues, and 40,000 pollinators.

This is her first book.

WEBSITE
uproarcoaching.com

LINKEDIN
linkedin.com/in/kari-ginsburg

INSTAGRAM
instagram.com/uproar_coaching

www.ingramcontent.com/pod-product-compliance
Lightning Source LLC
Chambersburg PA
CBHW051634120626
46551CB00014B/2076